Charles Henry Benjamin

Notes on mechanical laboratory Practice

Charles Henry Benjamin

Notes on mechanical laboratory Practice

ISBN/EAN: 9783337106355

Printed in Europe, USA, Canada, Australia, Japan

Cover: Foto ©ninafisch / pixelio.de

More available books at **www.hansebooks.com**

NOTES ON

Mechanical Laboratory Practice

—BY—

C. H. BENJAMIN

*Professor of Mechanical Engineering,
Case School of Applied Science.*

CLEVELAND
CHARLES H. HOLMES,
2303 EUCLID AVE.
1898.

PREFACE.

This book has been prepared for the use of students in connection with their work in the mechanical laboratory and contains descriptions of the more common apparatus used, directions for its care and use and forms for logs and reports of various experiments.

The experience of the writer has shown that much better results are secured by having a definite routine in laboratory work and by using printed forms for all logs and reports.

It is intended that duplicates of the forms given in the book shall be furnished to each division making an experiment and that these duplicates shall be filled out and handed in as a report of the conduct and results of the experiment, while the forms in the book itself can be filled out as a record for each student.

The duplicates all being of standard size, 6 × 9 inches, can be filed in envelopes and will constitute a permanent record of the tests made in the laboratory which may be of considerable value.

This book is not intended to take the place of the larger and more complete works on this subject which should be in the reference library of every laboratory, but as a hand book of convenient size to be taken into the testing room and used by the student in the conduct of experiments.

CONTENTS.

Chapter 1.

THE STRENGTH OF MATERIALS :
    The testing machine. Extensometers and other measuring instruments.
    Forms of specimens. Routine for various tests and forms for reports... 3—14

Chapter 2.

DYNAMOMETERS :
    Absorption and transmitting dynamometers. Alden dynamometer. Webber dynamometer. Belt testing machine. Calibration of dynamometers directions for use and forms for reports .... 15—31

Chapter 3.

MEASUREMENT OF HEAT AND STEAM :
    Thermometers, pyrometers, draft and steam gauges. Calibration of apparatus. Barrel calorimeter. Throttling calorimeter. Separating calorimeter. Barrus calorimeter. Forms for repor s .... 32—52

Chapter 4.

THE TESTING OF STEAM BOILERS :
    Equivalent evaporation. Table of factors. Standard method of making a boiler test. Simple forms for ordinary trials .... 53—66

Chapter 5.

INDICATORS AND PLANIMETERS :
    Directions for the care of indicators and their calibration. Reducing motions. Directions for the use of indicators. Theory of the polar planimeter and directions for its use. Indicator diagrams .... 67—79

Chapter 6.

TESTING STEAM ENGINES :
    Instruments. Test of surface condenser. Directions for making an engine test and forms for reports. Standard method for duty trials of pumping engines. Testing small pumps. Tables .... 80—104

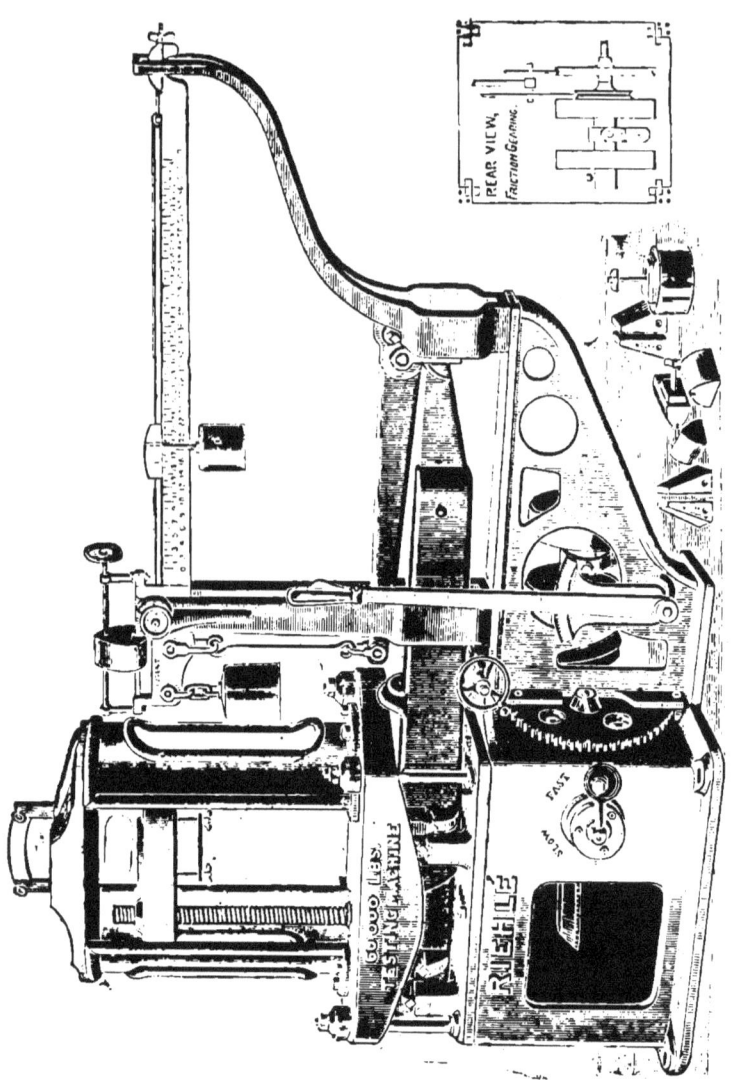

Fig. 1.

Chapter 1.

THE STRENGTH OF MATERIALS.

The Testing Machine.

The testing machine consists of the weighing device and the machinery for producing the pressure on the specimen.

The weighing device is similar to a platform scale. The platform rests upon a system of knife edges and levers connected with the weighing beam and is otherwise independent of the frame of the machine. In the machine shown in Fig. 1, the pressure mechanism consists of a pair of vertical screws, driven by a train of gears at speeds which can be varied at the will of the operator, and moving a cross-head up and down.

This crosshead transmits the pressure through the specimen in various ways to the weighing platform.

Directions for Use.

Balance the machine before making an experiment by moving the counterpoise on the inner end of beam, first slacking the nuts which prevent the platform from jumping off the knife edges. After balancing, the nuts may be screwed down with the fingers alone.

Notice all the oil holes in the machine and see that it has been properly oiled. If the beam is not sensitive enough raise the counterpoise; if too sensitive lower it.

Use the fastest speed for setting the machine, the slowest for testing hard, brittle materials and the intermediate for testing ductile materials such as soft steel, leather, etc. Do not reverse the lower speed lever when the machine is running. Practice reading the vernier before making an actual test.

Always stop the machine after completion of test to avoid danger of accident.

The Extensometer.

The extensometer is an instrument for measuring the distortion of a specimen exposed to tension or compression.

As the distortion in such cases is usually very small within the elastic limit, it is necessary to multiply it so that it can be easily measured.

The extensometer shown in Fig. 2 is the invention of the writer and is as simple as any. It consists of two vertical bars connected together by round studs at one side, the studs being provided with thumb nuts for closing the bars together and with spiral springs for separating them. Each bar is provided at the lower end with a steel point to bear on the specimen and at the upper end with a light steel lever in a horizontal position.

Each lever is provided with a steel point similar to those on the bars, and is so pivoted to the bar as to allow a limited vertical movement of the point.

As shown in the dotted lines in the figure, one lever is of the first and one of the third order, so that a slight vertical movement of the points will raise the outer end of one lever and depress that of the other through a greatly magnified distance. To the outer end of one lever is attached a graduated scale, over which the end of the second lever moves showing the stretch of the specimen.

The scale is so graduated as to read to ten-thousandths of an inch per inch of length of specimen, so that no dividing is necessary to get the unit strain.

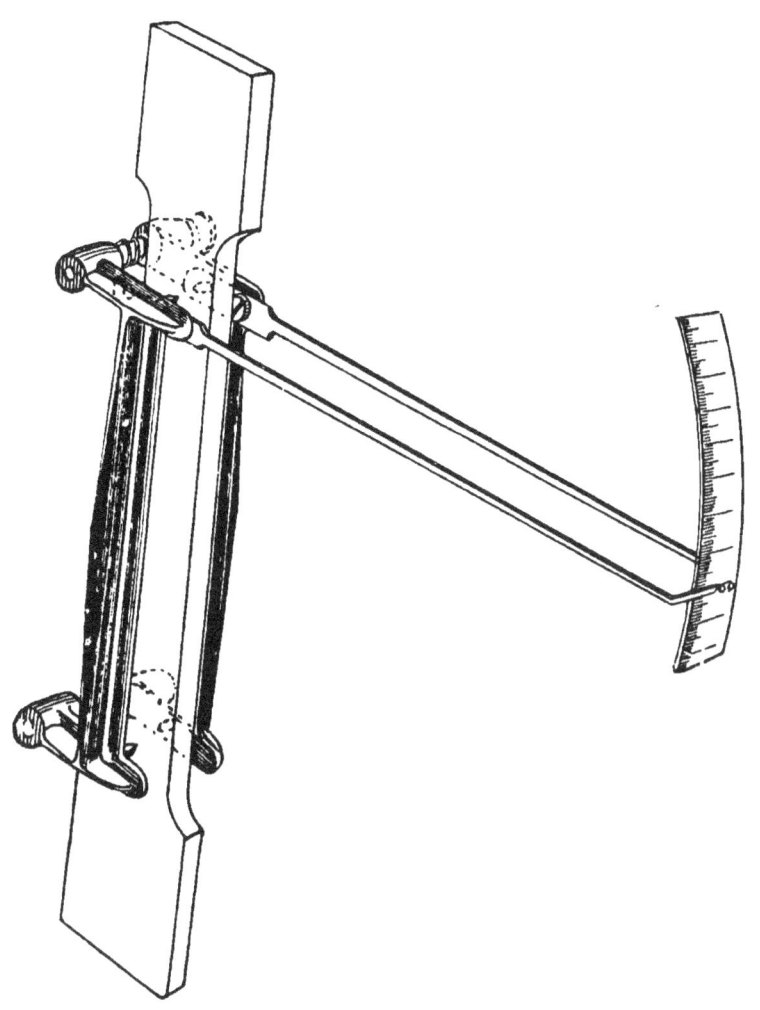

Fig. 2.

Directions for Use.

Mark the test specimen with the tram which accompanies the instrument, care being taken to have the marks central and exactly opposite each other. Apply the instrument after the specimen is in the machine, clamping first the points at the lower end, the instrument being in the position shown in Fig. 2 with the scale towards the operator.

Lift the levers until horizontal and turn the upper nut carefully until both points enter marks on specimen. See that the levers are not sprung too much and that the instrument reads nearly zero.

The instrument should be removed before rupture of the specimen.

The Autographic Extensometer.

Some extensometers have a pencil attachment which draws a strain diagram as the test progresses.

A modification of the instrument described in the preceeding article has attached to its frame a rotating cylinder or drum, carrying a piece of section paper, as in the steam engine indicator. This drum receives its rotary motion from a train of gears driven by the hand wheel which moves the poise of the machine.

On this instrument there is but one lever and this carries at its outer end a pencil point which moves up as the specimen stretches.

A curve is thus traced on the paper whose abscissae represent the successive loads applied and whose ordinates represent the corresponding elongations.

The advantage of an autographic diagram is that it is free from errors of observation. The disadvantage that, unless all test pieces are of the same size, the different curves cannot be compared as the loads are not reduced to stress per square inch.

Directions for Use.

Apply the instrument in the same manner as the other, except that the marks are now on the edges of a flat specimen instead of the side.

After connecting the worm shaft on the drum with the gears on the machine, adjust the pencil to the right height on the paper and draw a zero line making marks at intervals of a thousand pounds to show the horizontal scale.

In making the test be sure to keep the scale beam always floating.

The Deflectometer.

As its name implies the instrument shown in Fig. 3 is used for measuring the deflection of the specimen at the center when making transverse tests. The instrument is placed on the platform of the machine in such a way as to bring the adjusting screw under the center of the test bar.

The pointer is set at zero when there is no load on the specimen and when the load is applied the deflection in hundredths of an inch may be read directly from the graduated arc. Possibly greater accuracy may be insured by having the deflectometer attached directly to the supports of the test bar, but this instrument satisfies all the demands of ordinary practice.

Measurement of Specimens.

Particular care should be taken in the measurements of the cross-section of test specimens, since a small error here is more serious than if made in the reading of the vernier on the scale beam.

The micrometer caliper shown in Fig. 4 is well adapted to this purpose. Note that the longitudinal graduations on the barrel read: 0. .025 .05 .075 etc. while those on the rotary thimble represent thousandths of an inch. This particular micrometer has also on the back of the barrel a vernier which permits of the reading to ten-thousandths.

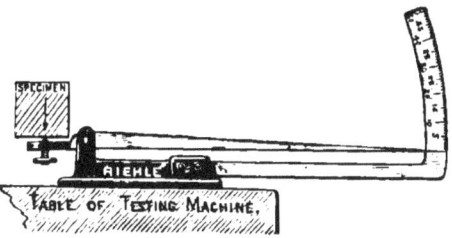

Fig. 3.

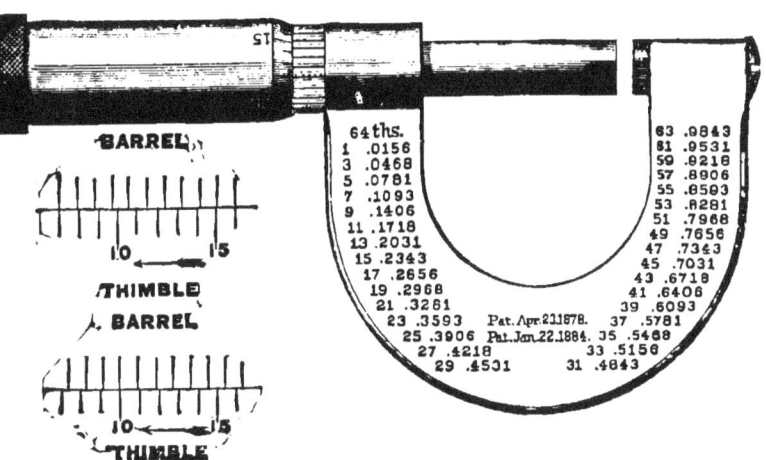

Fig. 4.

Remember always before using the caliper to set it at o and determine if it is correctly adjusted.

Form of Test Specimens.

The forms recommended for tension specimens by a committee of the American Society of Mechanical Engineers are shown in Figs. 5 and 6.

For cast iron it is necessary to have some form of universal joint at each end to insure freedom from oblique stress.

Fig. 7 shows the form adopted by the writer for belting tests.

Compression specimens are simple cylinders, 0.8 inches in diameter and sixteen inches long if to be used with an extensometer. Two inches of length is sufficient for a simple crushing test. Great care must be exercised to have the ends true and square.

For transverse tests of cast iron, bars are to be one inch square and twelve inches between supports for standard tests.

Other shapes and sizes may be used for special investigations.

If the specimen is cast in a horizontal position, the cope side should be placed uppermost in testing.

Tension Tests.

Directions:

Examine the surface of the specimen and see that it is free from nicks, flaws or tool-marks.

Measure it carefully as to breadth and thickness. Mark the centre line of the specimen if flat, and locate points for attaching extensometer.

Balance the machine and set specimen in jaws in a truly vertical and central position.

Attach extensometer, (see p. 5).

Calculate probable load at elastic limit and also ultimate load. Start the machine at slow speed and if possible take readings of extensometer without stopping the machine, at intervals corresponding to about one tenth load at elastic limit. If this is not practicable then stop the machine after each increment of load, balance the beam and take readings.

Remove the extensometer soon after reaching the elastic limit; this latter may be determined by the rapid movement of the extensometer point.

After this, keep the beam floating and note carefully the maximum load. The final breaking load may or may not be taken.

Remove the pieces from the machine, determine the total elongation by placing the pieces together and measuring between marks; caliper the contracted area at point of rupture and note character and location of fracture.

The accompanying forms show the character of log and report.

The determination of the elastic limit in ductile materials is attended with some difficulty since the rate of stretch increases almost from the beginning.

The so-called yield point or breaking down point where there is a sudden change in the rate of stretch can then be used instead, but even this is sometimes difficult to locate.

If the autographic extensometer is used no other strain diagram need be drawn.

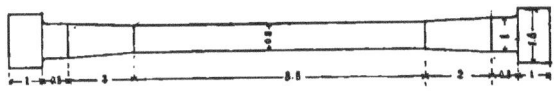

Fig. 5.

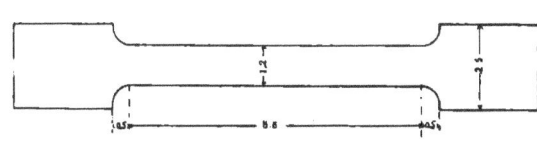

Fig. 6.

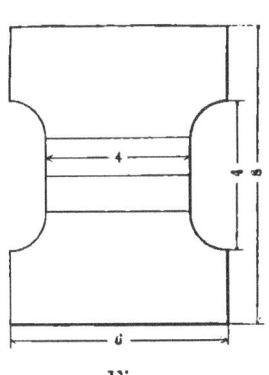

Fig. 7.

TESTING LABORATORY.   Date ....
    FORM A.

          LOG OF................... ....TEST.

     Mark...................... ....Material............................
     Shape....................Length between marks.....................
     Breadth........................Thickness....................... ......
     Observers...................... ....

Loads.		Extensometer.		Remarks.
Total=P	Per sq. in. =S	1st.	2nd.	

     Maximum load......................Final length....................... _
     Final breadth....... ....Final thickness.................
     Appearance of fracture.

TESTING LABORATORY.   Date..........................
    FORM B.

        REPORT OF........................TEST.
    By..
    For ....

Mark................ ....Material............................

Manufactured by... .

Shape ....Dimensions........................

Original Area............... ,.........	Original Length................... ....
Contracted Area.....................	Final Length...........................
Contraction.....................	Elongation ....,.............
% Contraction...................	% Elongation....:......... ....
Maximum Load......................	Load at El. Limit....................
Maximum Stress.....................	Stress at El. Limit ....
Character of Fracture..............	Elongation at El. Limit.............
Chem. Analysis by........	Resilience at El. Limit..............
	Increment of Stress...................
Carbon..........Phosphorus.........	Increment of Strain..................
Manganese..........Sulphur.........	Modulus E..... ....
Remarks	Sketch of Fracture.

        Checked by... ....

Compression Tests.

With long specimens the method of procedure is the same as in tension tests, except that compression blocks are used instead of jaws.

Great care must be taken to have the specimen exactly centered in the machine that there may be no oblique stress. The amount of flexure should be determined if practicable. The same forms of log and report may be used as in tension tests.

With short specimens the deflectometer may be used between the compression blocks to measure the distortion.

Punching and Shearing Tests.

These tests require the use of special apparatus. The distortion of the specimen plate may be measured roughly with the deflectometer as explained in preceding paragraph.

The report should give the dimensions and character of the dies used, the thickness of plate, the ultimate load and stress per square inch, and a curve should be plotted from which the elastic limit, the modulus of elasticity and the resilience may be determined.

Transverse Tests.

This is the form of test most satisfactory for cast iron and for brittle materials generally.

Directions.

Examine test bar carefully and note flaws. If cast in a horizontal position, mark cope side to be placed uppermost in testing. At one side mark lines for points of support and for line of pressure.

Arrange supports and plunger on machine and lay test bar in position.

Usually supports will be 24 inches apart and the load at the center. See that the test bar lies squarely on supports and that the plunger strikes squarely on top, using thin pieces of metal or paper under supports to bring this about.

See that center lines of supports and plunger are parallel and at right angles to axis of test bar. Set deflectometer with screw directly under center of bar. Balance the machine. Apply load of two or three hundred pounds, then remove load and set deflectometer at zero. Calculate the probable breaking load. Put up shield to ward off flying fragments.

Run the machine at slowest speed without stopping, to about two thirds the breaking load, taking simultaneous readings of deflectometer and of vernier at about ten equal intervals.

Reverse the machine, remove all the load and note permanent set. Repeat the application of load taking readings as before and continue until the bar breaks.

Be careful to keep the beam floating and to note readings continually near the end. Note the appearance and location of fracture and measure breadth and depth at this point.

TESTING LABORATORY.　　　　Date ....
　　FORM C.

LOG OF TRANSVERSE TEST.

Mark............ .... Material............................ ....

Shape......... ....Length between supports = l............ ...

Breadth = b........ ....Depth = h............... ....

Observers....... ....

Loads.		Deflections.		Remarks.
Total = W	Modulus = S	Δ_1	Δ_2	

Set Load............... ....Set........... ....

Maximum Load................. ....Max. Deflection......... ....

Location of Fracture........................ ....

Appearance of Fracture....................... ....

TESTING LABORATORY.　　　Date..............................
　FORM D.

REPORT OF TRANSVERSE TEST.

By..

For ....

Mark ....Material........................

Manufactured by...

Shape ....Breadth..............Depth.............

Length between supports...

Max. Load........	Set Load........................
Max. Deflection....................	Deflection.......................
Modulus of Rupture...............	Set.............................
Resilience from ⎱	Elastic Deflection...... ....
curve　⎰	Modulus E.........................

Formulas.	Formulas.
Rectangle : $S = \dfrac{3Wl}{2bh^2}$	Rectangle : $E = \dfrac{W'l^3}{4bh^3 \triangle'}$
Circle : $S = \dfrac{5.1Wl}{2d^3}$	Circle : $E = \dfrac{W'l^3}{2.35d^4 \triangle'}$

Remarks on Fracture.	Chemical Analysis by
	....
	Carbon......... Phosphorus.........
	Silicon...........Sulphur..... ....

Checked by..

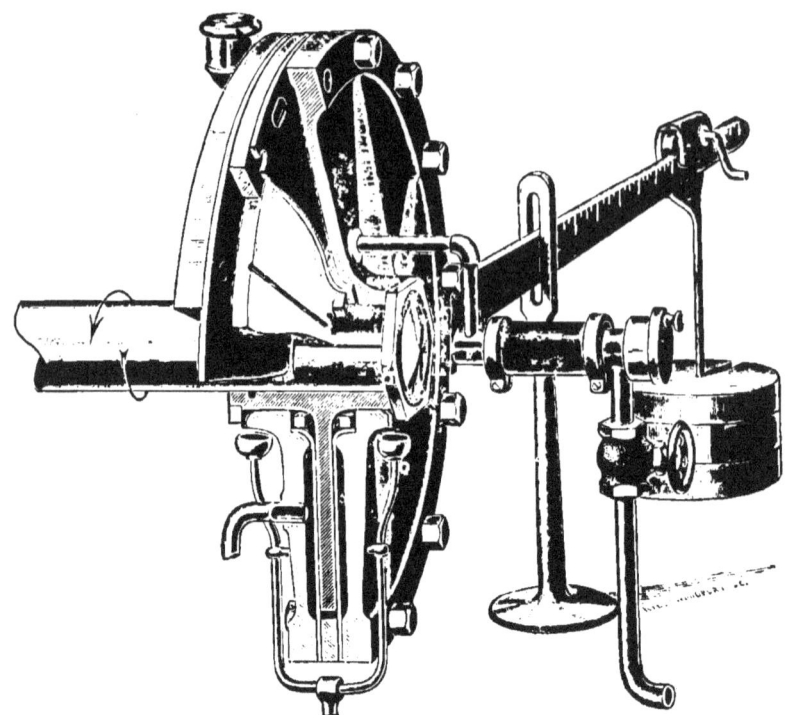

Fig. 9.

Chapter 2.

DYNAMOMETERS. *

Absorption Dynamometers.

Absorption dynamometers are those in which all the energy is absorbed by some form of friction brake and converted into heat.

The so-called Prony brake is the most common form of absorption dynamometer and may be understood from Fig. 8.

It consists of a pulley P mounted on a shaft, which is driven by the motor to be tested either directly or by a belt.

This pulley is embraced by a brake B of some form which may be adjusted to any desired degree of pressure. Attached to the brake is a lever L which is supported at the outer end by a weighing scale. The heat generated by the friction is usually carried away by circulating water.

The moment of the scale pressure about the center of shaft must then equal the moment of friction, which we will call T

Let P = net pressure on scale
l = effective lever arm in inches
N = no. revolutions per minute

Then T = Pl

Machine Design (68) :—

$$HP = \frac{TN}{63025} = \frac{PlN}{63025}$$

If l is made 63 inches the formula reduces to —

$$HP = \frac{PN}{1000} \text{ nearly}$$

a very convenient form for use.

*For a complete discussion of subject see Flathor's "Dynamometors" Wiley & Sons.

The pulley and brake take many different forms, most of them designed with a view to the easy control of the circulating water. The rim of the pulley may be trough shaped inside retaining water by centrifugal force, the water being led to the wheel by pipes or hose and removed by a scoop inside.

Another brake pulley has a hollow rim and arms and the water is introduced and taken away through holes in the shaft.

Other designers prefer to have the water circulate through the brake itself, employing for that purpose hollow bands of metal which bear directly on the pulley. The bands may be flattened copper tubes, ordinary small steam pipe, or may be built up of sheet metal. When the bands are metal the pulley surface should be of wood.

The Alden Dynamometer.

Fig. 9, illustrates a special form of absorption dynamometer invented by Prof. Alden of Worcester.

The following description is taken from a circular published by the inventor: "The AUTOMATIC ABSORPTION DYNAMOMETER is a device for securing a perfectly steady and uniform load for any motor, and for accurately measuring that load. The load is produced by water pressure against copper plates, these plates being thus pressed against the sides of a disc revolving with the shaft. The copper plates are secured to an outer cast iron casing, there being a watertight compartment between the cast-iron and the copper plates.

The casing has a lever arm carrying weights which balance the friction between the revolving disc and the copper plates. The disc runs in a bath of oil. Enough water flows through the water compartments to keep the copper cool."

It is thus seen that the pulley in this form of brake is replaced by the revolving disc, and the ordinary hollow brake band by the copper plates and the cast iron casing. This dynamometer has an automatic regulating valve for controling the pressure of the water.

In determining the constant weight of lever arm in any dynamometer, attach a spring balance to the outer end, first raise the arm a few degrees and note reading of scale, then lower the arm the same amount and note reading again. The average of the two readings will be the weight without friction.

TESTING LABORATORY.   Date................ ,..................
FORM E.

REPORT OF TEST WITH.... ....BRAKE.

By..... ....

On ....Engine

| Diameter of Pulley..... ...... | Length of Lever.............. |
| Width of Face.................. | Weight of Lever.............. |

Duration of test, min................	Total water used lbs..............
Total No. of revs.	Water per minute ....
Revs. per minute	Initial temperature ....
Pressure on scale, lbs.............. .	Final temperature ....
Net pressure	Difference ....
Moment in.........	Heat units per min. ....
Brake horse power	Foot lbs. per min. ....
(Water) horse power	Horse power ....
Difference	

Remarks: Log of Temperatures.

Time.	Initial.	Final.

Checked by..... ....

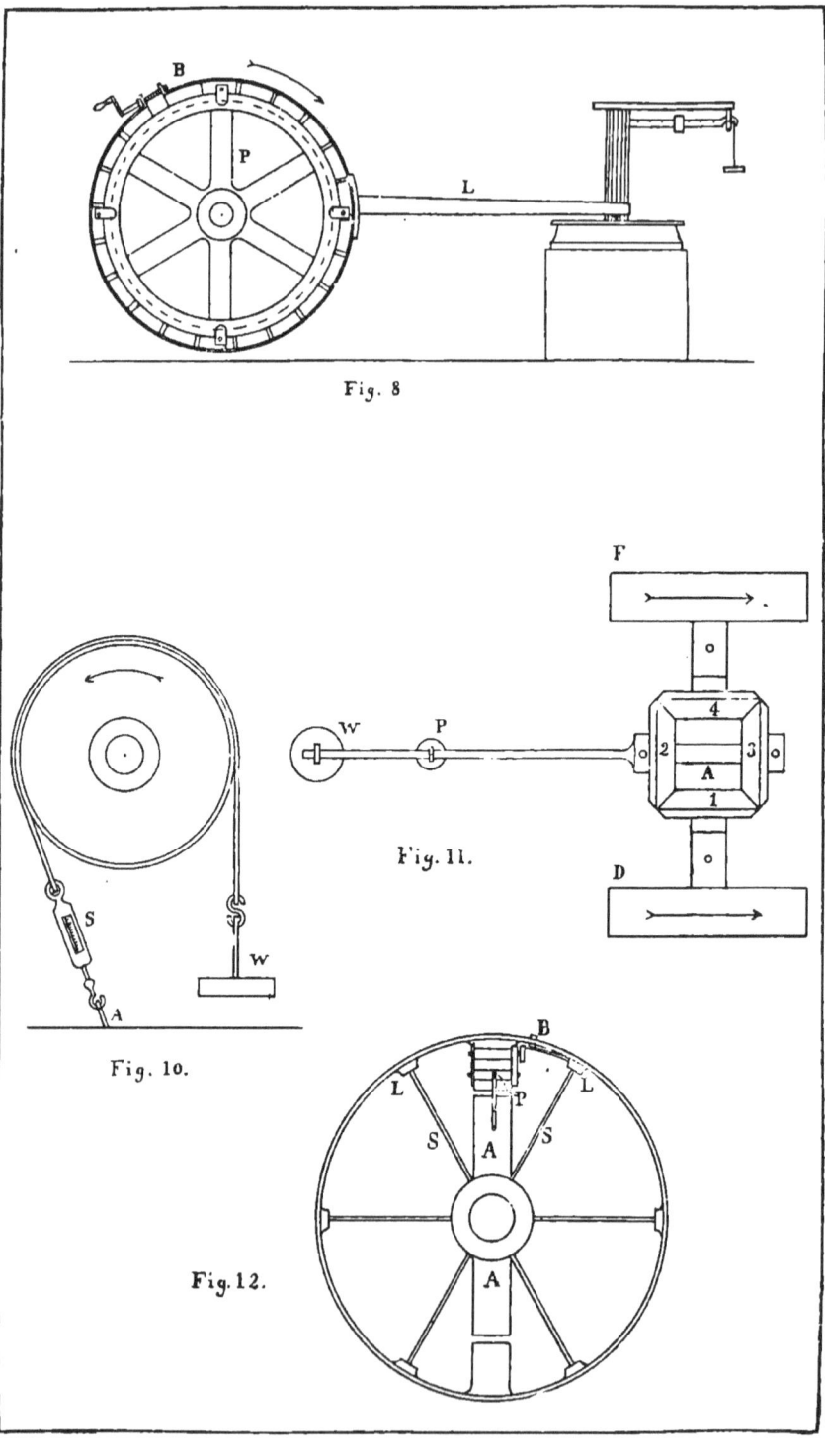

Fig. 8

Fig. 10.

Fig. 11.

Fig. 12.

Various forms of belt and rope brakes dispense with the brake lever and attach the weighing device directly to the flexible band. The belt brake is especially useful for light loads. As shown in Fig. 10, the weight W should be attached to the side of belt which has the greater tension, while the slack side is attached to the floor at A by a spring balance S.

By moving the fastening A the arc of contact of the belt may be increased or diminished at pleasure and the capacity of the brake thus regulated. The formula is the same as for the lever brake using the difference of tensions for P and the effective radius of pulley for l.

The rope brake is constructed on the same principle, only that in this case it is possible to make the arc of contact 360° or even more by carrying the end A Fig. 10 around and attaching to the ceiling.

The great advantages of the rope brake are its simplicity and cheapness, it being readily constructed out of materials at hand, and also the fact that it is so freely exposed to the air as not to heat quickly when in use.

Transmitting Dynamometers.

Transmitting dynamometers are those in which the power is transmitted to another shaft or machine instead of being absorbed by friction.

These dynamometers are used more particularly for measuring the power required to run different kinds of machines while absorption dynamometers are used to measure the power generated by prime movers.

The Webber Dynamometer.

One of the best known forms of transmitting dynamometers is the Webber the principle of which is shown in Fig. 11. The figure shows a top view of the working parts of the machine.

The pulley D is the driving pulley of the dynamometer

and receives power from outside. On the same shaft as D and rotating with it in the direction shown by the arrow is a mitre gear 1. This gear transmits the power through two idle gears 2 and 3 to the gear 4 which in turn drives the pulley F on the same shaft. The pulley F transmits the power by belt to the machine to be tested.

The shaft on which the idle gears rotate is free to turn in a vertical plane about the center A, the gears 2 and 3 rolling on the gears 1 and 4. When the dynamometer is in operation the shaft is prevented from turning by weights W, hung on an extension of the shaft in the form of a scale-beam.

It can readily be shown that the lifting moment on the scale-beam is double the moment transmitted by the machine.

Let T = moment transmitted in ft. lbs.
W = weight in scale pan.
l = lever arm of weight in ft.

Then $T = \dfrac{Wl}{2}$

and work done in one revolution of D is

$$2\pi T = \pi l W.$$

In the Webber dynamometer the bell rings once in one hundred revolutions

and $l = \dfrac{10}{2\pi}$ ft.

∴ Work per 100 revolutions $= \dfrac{1000 W}{2}$

A two pound weight is accordingly marked 1000 ft. lbs. and a five pound weight, 2500 ft. lbs.

A sliding poise P on the scale beam gives the readings between 1 and 1000.

Since the reading of the scale beam and weights gives directly the work in foot pounds per one hundred revolutions it is only necessary to divide the reading by the time in seconds of one hundred revolutions and by 550 to give the horse-power

or $$HP = \frac{W}{550t}$$

The additions of a dash-pot to steady the beam and of a counter shaft to bring driving and following pulleys in the same plane do not change the principle.

Directions for Use.

Set up the machine so that it is firm and level and bolt securely to the floor.

If possible belt from line shaft to upper pulley of dynamometer and from lower pulley to machine to be tested.

See that the driving pulley runs in the right direction to lift the scale beam, that the machine is well oiled and that all the oil cups are working freely.

Fill the dash-pot with thin oil or water and see that the nut in top of dash-pot does not clamp the rod. Arrange sight rod so as to show when scale beam is level.

Keep the scale beam level when testing and note the average load. After the conclusion of the test run the dynamometer with the belts on but with the second belt running on a loose pulley of the machine tested and thus get a friction reading which is to be deducted from the former readings before making calculations.

Calibration

In calibrating this dynamometer observe the above directions as to setting etc., but attach a Prony brake to the following pulley instead of a belt, and thus measure the net work done by the dynamometer.

The difference between the power indicated by the dynamometer and that shown by the brake will be the power consumed in friction of the dynamometer.

Make several runs with various brake pressures, but be

careful to maintain the pressure constant during each run.

Finally, determine the friction reading of the machine with the brake removed.

Weigh accurately the weights used in scale pan and the sliding poise, and measure the distance of notches and knife edge on scale beam from center of machine.

The following forms will serve for both log and report in these tests.

TESTING LABORATORY.   Date.........................
  FORM F.

REPORT ON CALIBRATION OF WEBBER DYNAMOMETER.

By ....

Dynamometer Constants:
Weight of Poise.................... of Weights...............
Radius of Knife-edge................of Zero-mark..............
Length of Graduated Scale..
Brake Constants:
Length of Lever............... Weight of lever................

No.	1	2	3	4	5
Duration of test in bells............					
Total time in seconds...............					
Total load on scales................					
Dynamometer reading......W......					
Time of 100 revs..............t......					
Dynamometer HP............D......					
Net brake load................P......					
Revs. per second............N.......					
Brake HP.......................B......					
Friction HP=D—B...............					
Per cent Friction $= \dfrac{D-B}{D}$					

Dynamometer formula: Brake formula:

$$HP = \frac{W}{550\,t}$$ $$HP = \frac{P\,l\,N}{1050}$$

Checked by..

TESTING LABORATORY.　　　　　Date..................................

FORM G.

　　　REPORT OF TEST ON..............................
　　　　　With Webber Dynamometer.

By..

For ....

Description and Dimensions of Machine.

....

....

....

Diameter of Dynamometer Pulley............................ins.

Diameter of Machine Pulley....................................ins.

. Kind of Belt...................... Width of Belt...............

No.	1	2	3	4	5
Duration of test in bells............					
Total time in seconds..................					
Time of 100 revs. in seconds=t..					
Work of 100 revs. in ft. lbs.=W					
Log W......................................					
Colog t.....................................					
Colog 550.................................					
Log total H.P............................					
Total H.P............................					
Friction H.P.......................					
Net H.P..............................					

Average H.P. from...............trials........................

　　　Checked by...

Spring Dynamometers.

A large class of transmitting dynamometers uses the deflection of a spring to register the moment transmitted. One of the simplest of these is the spring arm pulley.

Fig. 12 illustrates a dynamometer of this kind devised by the writer and used on a belt testing machine. A cast iron pulley rim two feet in diameter is furnished with twelve spring arms SS, cast into rim and hub. Each arm is of spring steel one inch wide and one eighth of an inch thick.

The cast iron arms AA are used in casting and finishing the pulley and are then cut so as not to interfere with the springing of the steel arms. To one of the arms A is fastened a recording pencil while the outer end of the same arm carries two rolls for cross section paper. The rolls are actuated by means of a train of gearing and a ratchet.

The ratchet is operated by a push button B moved by the pressure of the belt.

This pulley can be used on any shaft as a driving pulley and will record the moment transmitted. It may be calibrated by a brake or by hanging weights on the two ends of a belt passing over the pulley.

Belt Testing Machine.

To determine the power transmitted by leather belting under different conditions, a special machine must be arranged which shall not only show the power received and transmitted, but also the slip of the belt and the sum of the tensions on the two sides.

The belt machine used in the laboratory of the Case School of Applied Science is arranged as follows:

1. The pulley stand. This is a floor stand carrying a pulley for receiving the power from the line shaft and also the spring arm pulley to drive belt No. 1 and record the power received by that belt.

TESTING LABORATORY. Date......................
FORM H.

LOG OF BELT TEST.

Observers..

Kind of Belt....................Condition.......................

Made by...

Length.........feet   Width.........ins.   Thickness.........ins.

Machine Constants:

Circumference of Pulleys in feet, 1...... 2...... 3...... 4......

Weight of Bell Crank Arm......................................lbs.

Weight of Brake Arm...lbs.

Length of Brake Arm...ins.

Ratio of Brake Arm to Pulley Radius.............................

No.	1	2	3	4	5
Duration of test in bells............					
Total time in seconds..................					
Weighing Stand.					
First reading of counter.............					
Second reading of counter..........					
Total number of revolutions........					
Load on scales in lbs.................					
Prony Brake.					
First reading of counter.............					
Second reading of counter..........					
Total number of revolutions.......					
Load on scales in lbs.................					

2. The weighing stand. This stand carries a bell crank having vertical and horizontal arms. The vertical arms support a shaft carrying a pulley at each end and free to revolve. Pulley No. 2 receives belt No. 1 and transmits the turning moment along the shaft to Pulley No. 3 which drives belt No. 2.

Belts Nos. 1 and 2 lead off in the same direction from the bell crank and by their combined tensions press the horizontal arm of the bell crank down upon a platform scale, thus recording the sum of the tensions.

3. The Prony brake. This finally receives belt No. 2 and records the power delivered by the belts.

The shaft on first stand is provided with a gong which rings once for every hundred revolutions of the shaft.

The other two shafts are provided with counters to show the slip of belts.

Directions for Use.

Put paper on recording apparatus of spring pulley and get zero reading with belt off. Weigh bell crank arm and arm of Prony brake to get tare. Put on belts and then turn adjusting screws on weighing stand until belts are as tight as desired. See that bearings are well oiled. Set scales of Prony brake for desired load. Start up machine and adjust brake strap until scales balance. Note counters and see if slip is excessive; if it is, tighten belts until slip is reduced.

Run the machine for five bells, reading all counters at each bell and keeping both scales balanced by moving sliding poise. Do not adjust or oil Prony brake during the run. Note average loads on each scale. Stop the machine, remove belts and get zero mark again on diagram of spring pulley.

Repeat the experiment with increase of load and of tension
For formulas see *Notes on Machine Design pp.* 80-85.

TESTING LABORATORY. Date ....
FORM I.

REPORT OF BELT TEST.

By ....

Kind of Belt.......................Condition.........................
Made by........ ....

Length.........feet. Width..........ins. Thickness..........ins.

No.	1	2	3	4	5
Speeds in feet per minute.					
Pulley No. 1					
Pulley No. 2					
First belt, average					
Slip of first belt					
Per cent of slip					
Pulley No. 3					
Pulley No. 4					
Second belt, average					
Slip of second belt					
Per cent of slip					
Tensions in pounds.					
Average $T_1 + T_2$					
First belt $T_1 - T_2$					
Second belt $T_1 - T_2$					

TESTING LABORATORY. Date..
FORM K.

REPORT OF BELT TEST (Continued).

No.	1	2	3	4	5
First Belt.					
Driving tension T_1	....	....	....	....	......
Slack tension T_2	....	....	....	....	......
Ratio of tensions $\frac{T_1}{T_2}$	....	....	....	....	......
Co-efficient of friction $= f$	....	....	....	....	......
Horse Power received	....	....	....	....	......
Second Belt.					
Driving tension T_1	....	....	....	....	......
Slack tension T_2	....	....	....	....	......
Ratio of tensions $\frac{T_1}{T_2}$	....	....	....	....	......
Co-efficient of friction $= f$	....	....	....	....	—
Horse power delivered	....	....	....	....	......

General Summary, Average of......................Trials.

	First Belt.	Second Belt.	Average.
Per cent of slip	....	....	....
Horse power received	....	....	....
Horse power delivered	....	....	....
Efficiency	....	....	....
Sq. feet per min. per HP	....	....	....
Maximum tension $= T_1$	....	....	....
Max. tension per inch width	....	....	....

Checked by..

The Cradle Dynamometer.

This form of dynamometer is very useful for testing the the torque or moment of electric generators of small size. The generator is suspended in a swinging cradle which is supported by knife edges coinciding with the axis of rotation of the armature.

The center of gravity of the apparatus is raised by sliding weights until the desired degree of sensitiveness is obtained. The cradle carries a horizontal scale beam for the attachment of weighing devices and is counterbalanced so as to be in equilibrium when the generator is not running. The belt to the pulley of the generator must be vertical to avoid side pull on the knife edges. When the generator is running the moment of the weighing device about the line of knife edges will equal the torque of the machine.

For descriptions of various other forms of dynamometers, the student is referred to Prof. Flather's book on this subject before mentioned.

Fig. 13.

Chapter 3.

Measurement of Heat and Steam.

Instruments:

Before making tests of any kind it is important to know that all the instruments used are reliable.

The instruments used in such experiments should all be calibrated either directly or by comparison with some standard instrument.

Thermometers.

The thermometers should all be graduated on the glass, and should be occasionally tested for the melting point and boiling point of water.

For measurement of temperatures in steam pipes, vertical thermometer wells of thin brass should be screwed into the pipe.

The well should extend half-way across the pipe and when in use should be partially filled with cylinder oil and stopped with a perforated cork to prevent radiation and evaporation.

For live steam the longer thermometers reading to at least 350°F are necessary, while for temperatures of feed water those reading to 200°F are more easily read.

Temperatures of hot wells are most readily obtained by enclosing the thermometer in a metal frame having a cup at the lower end to hold water over the bulb.

The thermometer and frame can then be removed from the well or tank while taking the reading.

Keep thermometers in the cases when not using, never subject them to sudden jars or to over-heating and always carry them right end up.

Pyrometers.

Pyrometers for measuring high temperatures may be divided into three general classes.

1. Metallic pyrometers, which depend for their operation on the difference in expansion of two metals. These are usually rather slow to respond and are not suited for very high temperatures.

2. Electric pyrometers, which depend for their operation on the variation in electric resistance of a metallic circuit with change of temperature.

These are difficult to calibrate at high temperatures, but respond quickly to sudden changes.

3. Calorimetric pyrometers, where the heat is determined by heating a ball of some substance, whose specific heat is known, to the temperature required and then dropping it into water.

If proper care is taken to prevent radiation from the metal and from the water this method will probably be the most satisfactory of all. The ball may be inclosed in porcelain or fireclay until it is dropped in the water, and the vessel containing the water should have non-conducting walls and cover.

Let
  w = weight of ball
  s = specific heat of ball
  x = temperature of ball in degrees Fahr.
  W = weight of water in calorimeter
  t_1 = initial temperature of water
  t_2 = final temperature of water

The amount of heat given up by the ball of metal is:
$$h = ws(x - t_2)$$
and the amount of heat received by the water is:
$$h' = W(t_2 - t_1)$$

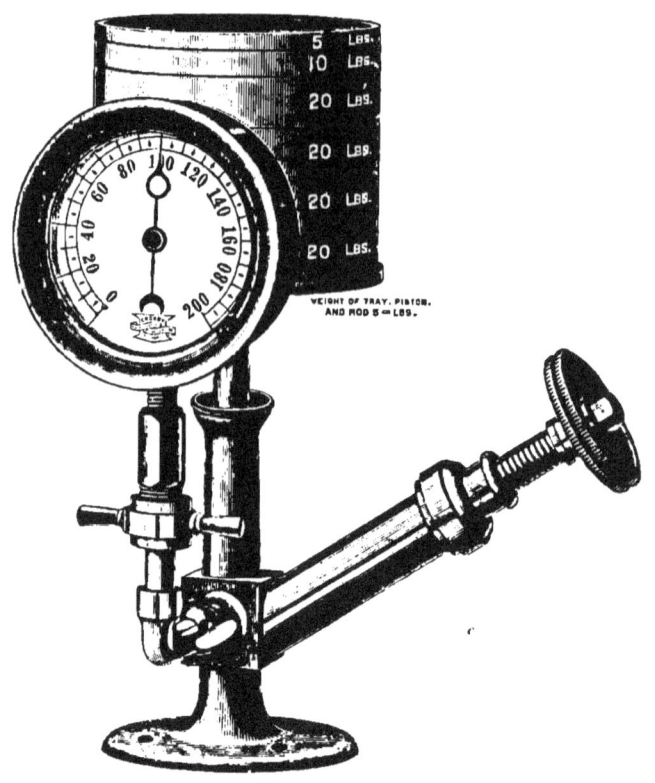

Fig. 14.

Putting these two amounts equal and solving for x we have :

$$x = \frac{W(t_2 - t_1)}{ws} + t_2$$

This method will also serve for the calibration of the ordinary pyrometer before mentioned.

Steam Gauges:

The ordinary Bourdon gauge Fig. 13 is almost universally used but needs to be frequently calibrated and adjusted.

The gauges used in a boiler test may be compared with some standard gauge known to be correct.

The test gauge itself however must be occasionally tested either with a mercury column or with some form of dead weight apparatus.

The objection to the mercury column is its inconvenience, its liability to be affected by changes of temperature and the fact that the specific gravity of the mercury used is not always the same.

One of the most convenient forms of dead weight testing apparatus is that shown in Fig. 14.

This apparatus has a vertical tube fitted with different couplings for the attachment of gauges to be tested.

Connected with this by a U tube is a vertical cylinder, having fitted to it a piston of exactly one-fifth of a square inch area. The piston rod carries a tray for weights, as shown in the figure.

The inclined tube furnishes an adjustable reservoir for oil.

Directions for Use.

The following directions for using the apparatus are given by the makers:—"Close the cock in the standard, withdraw the piston and turn out the screw plunger of the oil reservoir about one half or more of its length; then pour oil into the cylinder until it rises to within one inch of its top and insert the piston. Next, attach the gage to the standard and afterwards open the cock therein. The weight of the piston, rod and tray combined is exactly one pound, and will exert a pressure on the gage through the one-fifth square inch area of the piston of exactly five lbs. Now add weights—one at a time—and each will exert a pressure on the gage according to the number of pounds marked on it. As each weight is added revolve the piston with the weights gently, to insure perfect freedom of movement.

If in testing large gages more oil is needed, due to the descent of the piston under its weights, screw in the plunger until the piston has risen to its former height. Then proceed with the test by adding more weights. The weights ordinarily sent will test up to two hundred pounds pressure.

To get the oil back into the oil reservoir, unscrew the plunger and the weights will force the oil in the cylinder back; then by removing the weights, one at a time, the oil in the gage will also be forced back; close the cock, after which the gage and the piston may be removed."

The following form will be used for log and report of calibration.

TESTING LABORATORY.   Date..............................
    FORM L.

CALIBRATION OF STEAM GAUGE.

By..

For ....

No. of Gauge......................Capacity...................................

Made by..

Compared with ....

No.	Actual Load	Gauge.	Error.	Remarks.

Manometers.

For the measurement of small differences of pressure a mercury manometer is more accurate and more easily read.

In its simplest form this consists of a short U tube partially filled with mercury, one leg being open to the atmosphere and one connected by a rubber tube with the source of pressure. (See Fig. 16.)

The difference of level of the two columns of mercury is an index of the pressure. To reduce this to pounds per square inch divide the difference in level in inches by 2.036. This instrument can evidently be used as well for pressures below the atmosphere.

Draft Gauges.

It is always desirable to know the pressure as well as the temperature of the gases in the chimney when making a test of a boiler. The difference of pressure in this case is so slight that it is customary to use a manometer tube partially filled with water.

Fig. 15 shows a convenient form of this apparatus manufactured by Mahn & Co. of St. Louis.

It consists of the ordinary U tube half-full of water. One leg of the tube is connected to the chimney flue by a rubber tube attached at R. A three way cock H enables the observer to connect the tube with the chimney or with the open air at will. The leg A is always open to the air and has attached the micrometer screw T and the graduated scale I. In reading the gauge the cock H is first turned to admit the air when the level of the water in A is obtained by the screw. The cock is then turned to connect with the flue and the screw turned until its point again touches the water.

The difference of the readings of the micrometer multiplied by two will give the pressure of the draft in inches of water.

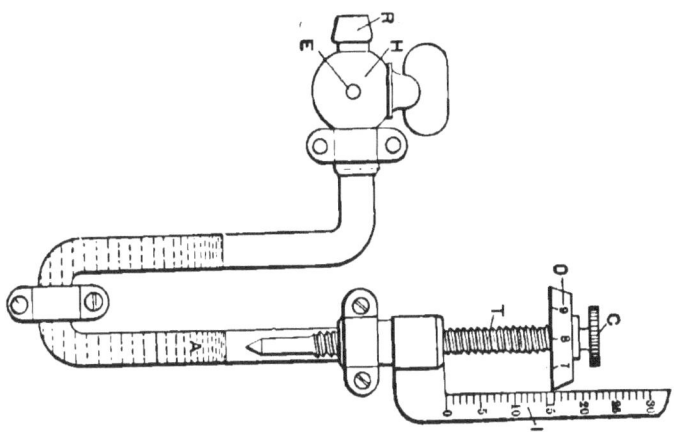

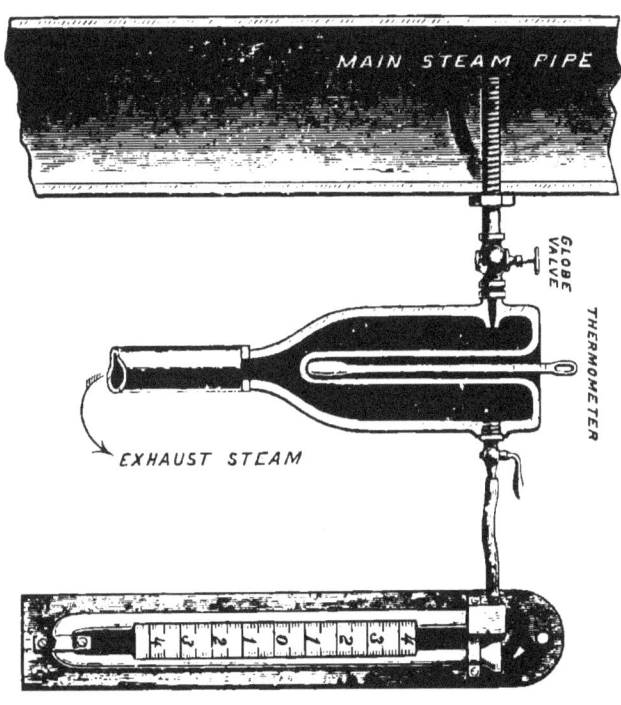

(See Heat and Steam p. 18.) To reduce this to pounds on the square foot, multiply by 5.21.

The point of the screw should be greasy, in order to prevent adhesion of the water.

Calorimetry

By calorimetry in this connection is meant the determination of the amount of moisture or condensation in steam.

In making an efficiency test of a boiler it is important that the boiler should be credited only with the amount of dry steam formed, and in the engine test it is equally important that the engine should not be charged with the water which comes over in the steam pipe.

Collection of Steam.

It may be said in the beginning that the most difficult problem is to get a fair sample of the steam. It is extremely doubtful if it is possible to do this with any great degree of accuracy when much water is present.

If there be only two or three per cent of moisture in the steam, as is ordinarily the case with good boilers and properly protected pipes, the water will be in minute drops and distributed throughout the steam if the pipe is vertical.

In a horizontal pipe most of the water will run along the bottom of the pipe and it will be difficult to obtain a fair sample. Furthermore it has been conclusively shown by experiments[*] that if the percentage of moisture be much greater than that indicated above, the water will not be evenly distributed in a vertical pipe but will move in sheets and streams in irregular manner, rendering it impossible to obtain a fair sample.

In such cases it is best to apply a separator to the under side of the horizontal pipe to remove the most of the water

―――――
*Trans. Am. Soc. Mech. Eng. Vol. XVI.

and then to test the steam by a calorimeter after it leaves the separator.

The best form of collecting tube is probably one which passes through a stuffing box in the pipe so that it may be adjusted in and out; in this case the tube would be open at the end and could be moved diametrically across the pipe so as to get samples from different sections.

Tubes extending three-fourths of the way across the pipe and perforated with small holes have been generally used, (see figs. 16 and 17) but it is probable that such tubes would themselves act to a certain extent as separators on account of the inertia of the water in the steam. The collecting tube should always be applied to a vertical pipe and preferably in an ascending current of steam.

The Barrel Calorimeter.

This, the oldest and best known form of colorimeter, consists of a barrel or other wooden tank resting on a platform scale and provided with a wooden cover. In some cases it is fitted with a rotary stirrer for mixing the water.

The barrel is partially filled with cool water whose weight and temperature are ascertained.

The steam whose quality it is desired to test is then led into the barrel by a hose and after a certain weight of steam has been condensed, the temperature of the mixture is ascertained:

Let
W = original weight of cool water
t_1 = initial temperature of water
t_2 = final temperature of water
q_2 = final heat of liquid
w = weight of steam injected
t = temperature of steam
q = corresponding heat of liquid
r = corresponding latent heat of evaporation
x = per cent of dry steam

The amount of heat given by the steam is then ;
$$h = wxr + w(q - q_2)$$
The amount of heat received by the water is:
$$h' = W(t_2 - t_1)$$
Putting these amounts equal and solving for x, we have :
$$x = \frac{W(t_2 - t_1)}{wr} - \frac{q - q_2}{r}$$

It is advisable to use q instead of t for the steam, since the specific heat is greater than unity at high temperatures.

See Peabody's Steam Tables.

Directions for Use.

Set the barrel on the scale and see that it does not touch other objects. Fill two-thirds full of cold water. Weigh accurately and determine t. Connect hose to steam pipe and blow steam through it enough to warm it thoroughly, then insert into the barrel under the water. Allow it to remain until the temperature of the water has risen to over 100°F and remove it with steam still blowing through it. The steam should not be turned on at full pressure except when the hose is in the barrel, as it would make the hose difficult to handle.

After removing the hose weigh the water and barrel carefully and determine the temperature t_2. A stirrer is usually not needed if the steam enters the water at full pressure. Empty all the water from the barrel and weigh the barrel. Neglect the results of this experiment as it is simply made to heat the apparatus.

Refill the barrel with cold water and proceed as before.

Repeat the experiment several times and average results.

Remember to weigh the empty barrel each time. The pressure and temperature of the steam should both be noted during each experiment.

This apparatus is not reliable for determining small amounts of moisture, as the probable error is too great.

The following form may be used for log and report.

TESTING LABORATORY. Date ....
FORM M.

REPORT OF CALORIMETER TEST.

By ....

For ....

Kind of Calorimeter........................... Weight ....

Steam from ....boiler

Used for..

No.	Symb'l	1	2	3	4	5
Barometer in room						
Temperature of room						
Duration of test in minutes						
First weight of water, lbs.						
Weight of calorimeter, lbs.						
Difference =	W					
Second weight of water lbs.						
First ,, ,, ,, ,,						
Difference =	w					
Final temp. of water Fahr.	t_2					
Initial temp. of water ,,	t_1					
Difference =	D					
Gauge pressure of steam =	p					
Temperature of steam =	t					
Heat of liquid at t	q					
Heat of liquid at t_2	q_2					
Difference =	d					
Heat of vaporization at t	r					
Per cent of dry steam	x					

Average of ....trials.   x = ...

Formula: $x = \dfrac{WD}{wr} - \dfrac{d}{r}$

The Throttling Calorimeter.

This form of calorimeter makes use of the fact that dry steam is superheated by throttling.

The steam to be tested is admitted through a small orifice into a chamber where the pressure may be regulated at will by manipulating an exit valve.

A manometer tube and inserted thermometer show the pressure and temperature in the chamber at each instant. The effect of the throttling at the entrance orifice is first to evaporate the entrained water and then if any surplus heat is left, to superheat the steam.

The degree of superheat then shows the dryness of the steam

If there is too much moisture in the steam it will not be superheated at all and this method cannot be used.

Let t = temperature of steam to be tested
q = corresponding heat of liquid
r = corresponding heat of evaporation
p_1 = pressure inside calorimeter
t_1 = corresponding temperature from tables
t_2 = actual temperature in calorimeter
H_1 = total heat of steam at t_1
x = per cent of dry steam in pipe

Then will $t_2 - t_1$ be the degrees of superheat caused by throttling, and if we assume 0.48 as the specific heat of the steam :

$0.48(t_2 - t_1)$ = heat units expended in superheating each pound

The heat in each pound of the mixture before throttling is : $h = xr + q$
and after throttling is $h' = H_1 + 0.48(t_2 - t_1)$
if the steam is superheated.

As no heat is received or rejected : $h = h'$

Putting these two amounts equal and solving for x:
$$x = \frac{H_1 - q + 0.48(t_2 - t_1)}{r}$$

The throttling calorimeter as manufactured by Schaeffer & Budenberg of New York is shown in Fig. 16 which needs no description.

Directions for Use.

Attach the calorimeter to the steam pipe as shown in the figure and open the globe valve wide, allowing the steam to blow through into the air or into a condenser.

Fill the thermometer cup with cylinder oil and introduce the thermometer. Attach the manometer having first filled it with mercury to the zero mark, and be sure that it is vertical. Allow steam to blow through the instrument for about ten minutes before taking readings. Then observe the temperature and pressure in the calorimeter and that in the steam pipe simultaneously. Reduce inches of water in calorimeter leg to inches of mercury by dividing by 13.6.

In all calorimeter tests it is advisable to have a recording steam gauge attached to the steam pipe and only take readings when the pressure of the steam is nearly constant. Gauges respond quickly to changes, while thermometers in cups do not. This is especially important with throttling calorimeters.

The throttling calorimeter is considered very reliable in cases where the moisture does not exceed three or four per cent at 90 lbs. gauge pressure.

The instrument is very convenient since it is continuous in its action and readings can be taken as often as desired.

The following form can be used for log and report.

TESTING LABORATORY.   Date..................................
   FORM N.

REPORT OF THROTTLING CALORIMETER TEST.

By ....

For..

Calorimeter made by...

Steam from........ ....boiler

Used for..

	Symb'l	1	2	3	4	5
Time		......	......	......	......	......
Temperature, main pipe	t	......	......	......	......	......
Guage pressure, main pipe	p	......	......	......	......	......
Barometer, inches		......	......	......	......	......
Manometer, inches		......	......	......	......	......
Total pressure, inches		......	......	......	......	......
Absolute pressure, lbs,	p_1	......	......	......	......	......
Temperature in Calorimeter	t_2	......	......	......	......	......
Temperature due to p_1	t_1	......	......	......	......	......
Degrees of Superheat	$t_2 - t_1$	......	......	......	......	......
Total heat at p_1	H_1	......	......	......	......	......
Heat of liquid at t	q	......	......	......	......	......
Latent heat at t	r	......	......	......	......	......
Per cent of dry steam	x	......	......	......	......	......

Average of..................trials. $x =$ ....

The Separating Calorimeter.

This form of calorimeter is shown in Fig. 17 as manufactured by Schaeffer & Budenberg. As its name implies, it measures the water in the steam by separating it mechanically and collecting the water in one chamber while the dry steam is condensed in another. The ratio of the two amounts gives at once the percentage of moisture in the steam, assuming that the separation is complete.

In the figure the steam passes into the calorimeter at K where it is obliged to pass downward and then upward through narrow orifices. The water is separated and falls to the bottom of the inner chamber, where it may be measured by the attached gauge glass N. The dry steam passes down the outer chamber F and into the condenser at J where it can be measured by means of the transparent scale. The steam forms a jacket to the inner chamber E thus preventing loss of heat by radiation.

The scale on the calorimeter is graduated to read to one hundredths of a pound at the ordinary temperature of the steam. That on the condenser reads to pounds and tenth at the temperature of 110°F.

Directions for Use.

The apparatus is arranged as shown, the connecting pipe being protected from radiation by some covering.

Fill the condenser to the zero-mark with cold water.

Disconnect the rubber tube R and allow steam to blow through the calorimeter, until the water reaches the zero mark on the gauge glass.

Connect the tube R to the condenser and begin the experiment. The run may be continued until the gauge glass becomes full or until the water in the condenser becomes too warm to proceed further. Note amount collected in calorimeter and in condenser. Empty condenser and fill as before with cold water.

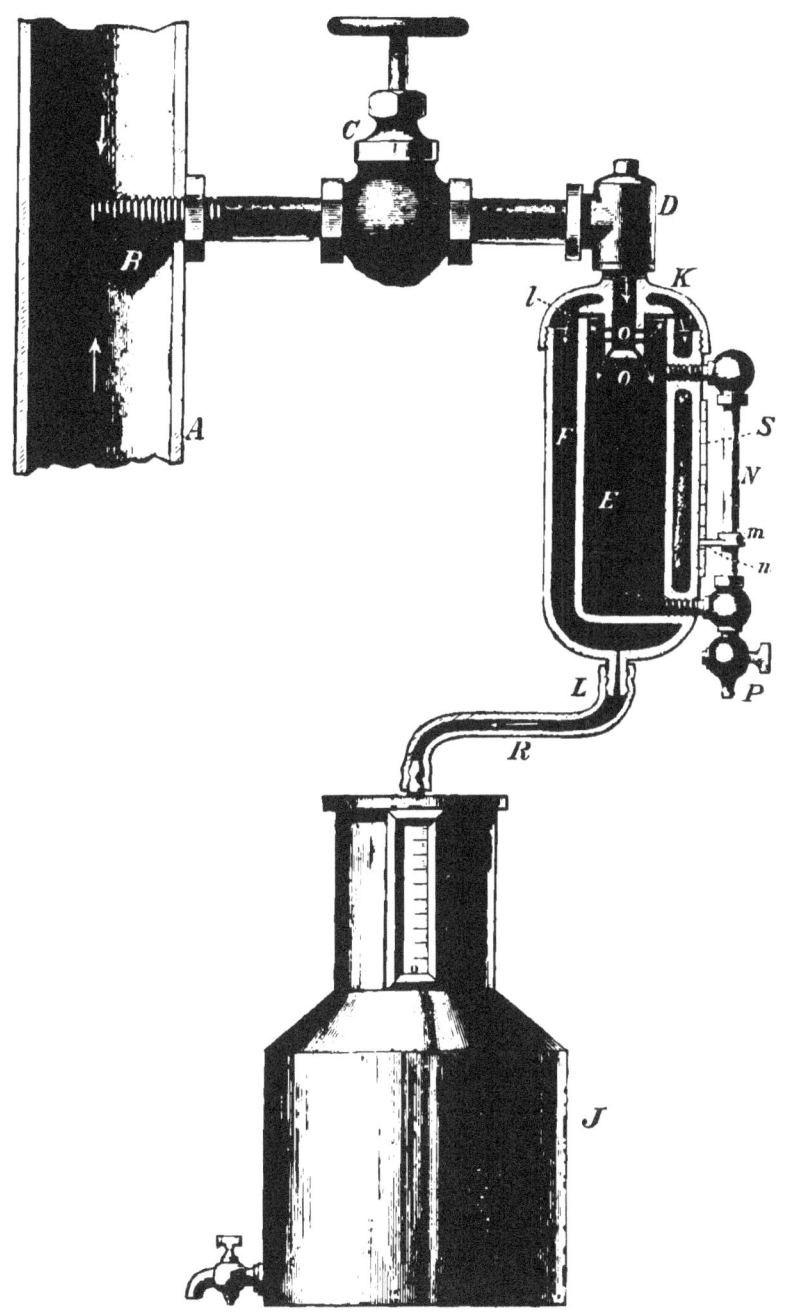

Fig. 17.

Draw water from gauge glass by cock at P until it reaches the zero mark. Repeat experiment as often as desired.

The advantages of this instrument are its simplicity and the ease with which the calculations are made.

The following form may be used for log and report of test.

TESTING LABORATORY. Date........ ....
FORM O.

REPORT OF SEPARATOR CALORIMETER TEST.

By ....

For..

Calorimeter made by..

Steam from........ ....boiler

Used for...

	Symb'l	1	2	3	4	5
Barometer in room						
Temperature in room						
Duration of test in minutes						
Gauge pressure, lbs.						
Absolute pressure, lbs.	P					
Weight of steam, lbs.	W					
Weight of water, lbs.	w					
Total weight of mixture	W+w					
Radiation Loss, lbs.	R					
Per cent moisture	1−x					
Per cent dry steam	x					

Average of.................trials.   x = ...

Formula : $1 - x = \dfrac{w - R}{W + w}$

Remarks on radiation:

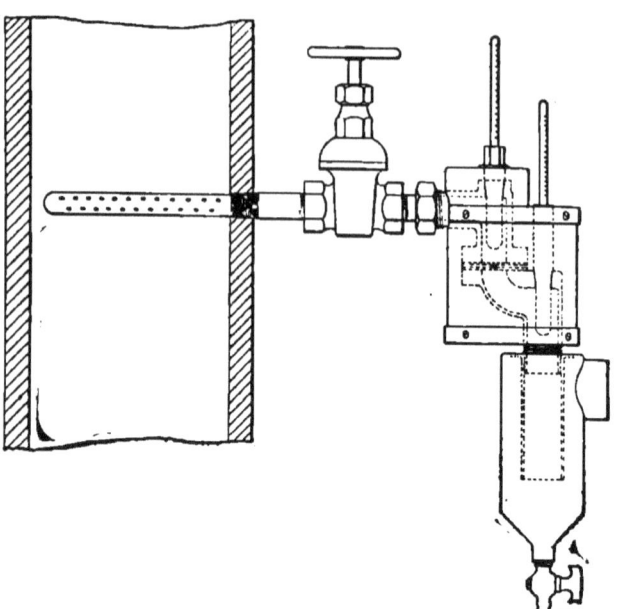

Fig. 18.

The Barrus Calorimeter.

Fig. 18 illustrates a combined throttling and separating calorimeter designed by Mr. Geo. H. Barrus and manufactured by Gowing and Co. of Boston.

As has been already explained the throttling calorimeter is only capable of measuring the moisture in steam when less than about four per cent is present. In the apparatus shown in the figure the separating device can be brought into action at any time, to measure the water not evaporated by the throttling.

The throttling part of this calorimeter is termed the heat gauge and consists of two chambers separated by a plate containing a circular orifice $\frac{3}{32}$ inches in diameter.

The two chambers are insulated from each other by non-conducting material and are suitably protected from loss of heat by radiation.

Each chamber is provided with a thermometer, the upper thermometer showing the temperature of the entering steam and the lower one the temperature after throttling.

The separator consists of a vertical chamber which the steam enters after passing through the heat gauge. If any water remains in the steam it will be precipitated to the bottom of the separator, while the steam passes out near the top.

The following directions for attaching and using the instrument are taken from a circular issued by the makers.

Directions for Attaching the Instrument.

Sec. 1. Connect the instrument to a straightway valve attached to the main steam pipe in the manner shown in the cut. Select a locality that will give an average sample of the steam to be tested. Use a half inch pipe extending across the full diameter of the main, and perforate the enclosed portion with 48 one-eighth inch holes, the extreme end being welded or plugged.

Sec. 2. Blow out the connecting pipe before attaching the instrument, so as to free the same from any dirt. If this is not done, the orifice may become obstructed, a fact which will reveal itself by the reduced quantity of steam passing through the instrument. It is important that the orifice be kept clear.

Sec. 3. Cover the connecting pipe with hair felting not less than three-fourths of an inch thick.

Sec. 4. Use cylinder oil in the two thermometer cups. Fill them one-third full, or sufficient to cover the bulbs of the thermometers.

Sec. 5. It is important that there should be no leak at any point about the apparatus, either in the stuffing box of the supply valve, the joints, or the union.

Directions for using the Heat Gauge alone.

Sec. 1. After the instument is thoroughly warmed, read the two thermometers at intervals of one minute for a continuous period of at least fifteen minutes duration. Find the average of these observations.

Sec. 2. Find the normal reading of the lower thermometer. Subtract from this the average reading of that thermometer obtained as pointed out in Sec. 1. This gives the number of degrees of cooling produced by the moisture.

Sec. 3. Divide the number of degrees of cooling found in Sec. 2 by the appropriate co-efficient obtained from the following table. (See Transactions A. S. M. E., Vol. XI., page 795 for particulars regarding the manner of obtaining these co-efficients.)

Temperature shown by upper thermometer Deg. Fahr.	Co-efficient.
280	21.8
300	21.5
320	21.1
340	20.8
360	20.5
380	20.2

The quotient obtained is the number of per cent of moisture.

Sec. 4. The normal reading is obtained by observing the lower thermometer when the fire in the boiler is banked, and little, if any, steam is passing through the main pipe. The pressure should be maintained at such a point that the upper thermometer indicates the average reading, as found in Sec. 1. The pressure should also be as nearly as possible constant, and the trial should be continued a sufficient time (usually half an hour) to establish a constant indication of the lower thermometer.

When the connection between the calorimeter and main pipe is short and well covered with hair felting, the normal readings for various cases are not far from the figures given in the following table:

Temperature shown by upper thermometer Deg. Fahr.	Approximate Normal Reading of lower thermometer Deg. Fahr.
280	250
290	256
300	262
310	263
320	274
330	280
340	286
350	292
360	298
370	304
380	310

Directions for using the Complete Instrument.

When the separator is brought into use, which will be required when the lower thermometer drops much below $214°$ the total percentage of moisture sought is divided into two parts The first part is that indicated by the heat gauge: while the second, or balance, is the moisture which escapes to the separator and is there removed.

The first part is determined in precisely the same manner as pointed out above. The second part is determined as follows:

Sec. 5. Collect the water dripping from the bottom of the separator in a bucket resting on scales (graduated to quarter ounces). Observe the weight every five minutes and continue the test for a period of at least half an hour. Find the weight of water collected during each five minute interval, and reduce each one to its equivalent hourly rate by multiplying by 12.

Sec. 6. Find the weight of water condensed per hour by radiation loss from the separator, and subtract this from the hourly weights found in Sec. 5. The remainders are the net quantities in the original steam which the heat gauge fails to indicate.

The radiation loss here referred to may be found by blowing steam through the instrument at such a slow rate that the lower thermometer indicates $215°$ to $217°$ (which must be done at some time when the boiler is making fairly dry steam) then collecting and weighing the water dropping from the separator, and calculating therefrom the hourly loss.

This loss amounts to approximately thirteen hundredths (0.13) of a pound per hour, when the surrounding temperature is $70°$.

Sec. 7. Divide the net quantities found in Sec. 9 by the quantity of steam and water passing through the calorimeter per hour. The results multiplied by 100 give the percentage of moisture shown by the separator corresponding to the successive five-minute observations. Find the average of these percentages.

Sec. 8. Add the percentages found in Sec. 7 to that computed from the heat-gauge readings (calculated as pointed out in Sections 1 to 4), and the sum is the total percentage of moisture sought.

Sec. 9. To find the quantity of steam and water passing through the instrument, attach a pipe to the side outlet and a rubber tube to the bottom nipple, and carry both to a tub of water resting on scales. Find the increase in weight for a period of say five minutes and multiply this by 12 to obtain the rate per hour.

For approximate work, the quantity can be determined from the following table, which shows the approximate amount of steam discharged through an orifice three thirty-seconds of an inch in diameter (the standard size used in this instrument for pressures under 150 lbs.) corresponding to various temperatures indicated.

Temperature shown by upper thermometer Deg. Fahr.	Steam discharged per hour through orifice 3-32" diam. lbs.
280	17.5
300	23.8
320	31.8
340	41.9
360	54.3
380	69.4

Explanations.

The reasoning used in determining the co-efficients given in Sec. 3 is as follows:

First suppose the steam to be dry on entering and its total heat to be $= H$. Its temperature after throttling will depend on the back pressure and will be what is termed in Sec. 2 the normal temperature.

For instance if the back pressure is equal to that of the atmosphere, the total heat of saturated steam at that pressure is 1146 t.u.

Consequently $H - 1146$ heat units have been expended in superheating and if we assume .48 as the specific heat the rise of temperature above $212°$ will be $\frac{H-1146}{48}$.

Secondly, suppose that the entering steam contains one per cent of moisture. Its total heat is then $H - \frac{r}{100}$ and there is less heat available than before by the amount $\frac{r}{100}$.

The number of degrees of superheat will accordingly be less than in the first instance by the amount $\frac{r}{100 \times .48} = \frac{r}{48}$ and this last will be the difference between the actual temperature by the lower thermometer and the so-called normal temperature, for each one per cent of moisture in the entering steam and is therefore the co-efficient in Sec. 3.

It is proper to say that Mr. Barrus prefers to use values of the specific heat varying from .42 to .51, according to the temperatures, these values having been determined by experiment with this same apparatus.

The following form may be used for log and report of test.

TESTING LABORATORY.   Date..................................
    FORM P.

REPORT OF TEST WITH BARRUS CALORIMETER.

By..

For..

Calorimeter made by..

Steam from...boiler

Used for..

Heat Gauge.

Readings, upper thermometer

Readings, lower thermometer

Average temperature of upper chamber ....

Average temperature of lower chamber................................

Normal temperature of lower chamber..................................

Number degrees of cooling..

Value of co-efficient used...

Percentage of moisture in heat gauge...................................

Separator.	1	2	3	4	5	6
Water lbs.						
Rates per hour						
Radiation per hour						
Net rates per hour						
Steam and water per hr.						
Percentages of moisture						

Average by separator

Total percentage of moisture

Chapter 4.

THE TESTING OF STEAM BOILERS.

The object of testing a steam boiler is usually to find the amount of water it is capable of evaporating for each pound of coal burned on the grate under certain specified conditions.

The usual standard of evaporation is called the "equivalent evaporation from and at 212°F per pound of dry coal." This means the amount of water which would be evaporated by each pound of dry coal, if the feed water were supplied at 212° and evaporated at the same temperature. The heat required for each pound of water would then be simply the latent heat of evaporation at 212°F or 966 t.u.

The equivalent evaporation is found by multiplying the actual evaporation by a factor of evaporation. This factor is the ratio of the actual heat required per pound of steam under the existing conditions to the number 966.

Let t = actual temperature of steam
r = corresponding heat of evaporation
q = corresponding heat of liquid
t_1 = temperature of feed water
q_1 = corresponding heat of liquid
e = factor of evaporation

Then will:
$$e = \frac{r + q - q_1}{966}$$

The following table of factors of evaporation is taken from "Steam Making" by Prof. Chas. A. Smith.

FACTORS OF EVAPORATION.—Pressure in Pounds per Square Inch above the Atmosphere.

Temperature of Feed-water in Degs. Fahr.	0	5	10	15	20	25	30	35	40	45	50	60	70	80	90	100	120	140	160	180	200
35	1.184	1.189	1.192	1.196	1.198	1.201	1.203	1.206	1.208	1.209	1.211	1.214	1.216	1.219	1.221	1.224	1.228	1.231	1.234	1.236	1.238
40	1.179	1.184	1.187	1.191	1.193	1.196	1.198	1.201	1.203	1.204	1.206	1.209	1.211	1.214	1.216	1.219	1.223	1.226	1.229	1.231	1.233
45	1.173	1.178	1.181	1.185	1.187	1.190	1.192	1.195	1.197	1.198	1.200	1.203	1.205	1.208	1.210	1.213	1.217	1.220	1.223	1.225	1.227
50	1.168	1.173	1.177	1.180	1.182	1.185	1.187	1.190	1.192	1.193	1.195	1.198	1.200	1.203	1.205	1.208	1.212	1.215	1.218	1.220	1.222
55	1.163	1.168	1.171	1.175	1.177	1.180	1.182	1.185	1.187	1.188	1.190	1.193	1.195	1.198	1.200	1.203	1.207	1.210	1.213	1.215	1.217
60	1.158	1.163	1.166	1.170	1.172	1.175	1.177	1.180	1.182	1.183	1.185	1.188	1.190	1.193	1.195	1.198	1.202	1.205	1.208	1.210	1.212
65	1.153	1.158	1.161	1.165	1.167	1.170	1.172	1.175	1.177	1.178	1.180	1.183	1.185	1.188	1.190	1.193	1.197	1.200	1.203	1.205	1.207
70	1.148	1.153	1.156	1.160	1.162	1.165	1.167	1.170	1.172	1.173	1.175	1.178	1.180	1.183	1.185	1.188	1.192	1.195	1.198	1.200	1.202
75	1.143	1.148	1.151	1.155	1.157	1.160	1.162	1.165	1.167	1.168	1.170	1.173	1.175	1.178	1.180	1.183	1.187	1.190	1.193	1.195	1.197
80	1.137	1.143	1.146	1.149	1.151	1.154	1.156	1.159	1.161	1.162	1.164	1.167	1.169	1.172	1.174	1.177	1.181	1.184	1.187	1.189	1.191
85	1.132	1.137	1.140	1.144	1.146	1.149	1.151	1.154	1.156	1.157	1.159	1.162	1.164	1.167	1.169	1.172	1.176	1.179	1.182	1.184	1.186
90	1.127	1.132	1.135	1.139	1.141	1.144	1.146	1.149	1.151	1.152	1.154	1.157	1.159	1.162	1.164	1.167	1.171	1.174	1.177	1.179	1.181
95	1.122	1.127	1.130	1.134	1.136	1.139	1.141	1.144	1.146	1.147	1.149	1.152	1.154	1.157	1.159	1.162	1.166	1.169	1.172	1.174	1.176
100	1.117	1.122	1.125	1.129	1.131	1.134	1.136	1.139	1.141	1.142	1.144	1.147	1.149	1.152	1.154	1.157	1.161	1.164	1.167	1.169	1.171
105	1.111	1.117	1.120	1.123	1.125	1.128	1.130	1.133	1.135	1.136	1.138	1.141	1.143	1.146	1.148	1.151	1.155	1.158	1.161	1.163	1.165
110	1.106	1.111	1.114	1.118	1.120	1.123	1.125	1.128	1.130	1.131	1.133	1.136	1.138	1.141	1.143	1.146	1.150	1.153	1.156	1.158	1.160
115	1.101	1.106	1.109	1.113	1.115	1.118	1.120	1.123	1.125	1.126	1.128	1.131	1.133	1.136	1.138	1.141	1.145	1.148	1.151	1.153	1.155
120	1.096	1.101	1.104	1.108	1.110	1.113	1.115	1.118	1.120	1.121	1.123	1.126	1.128	1.131	1.133	1.136	1.140	1.143	1.146	1.148	1.150
125	1.091	1.096	1.099	1.103	1.105	1.108	1.110	1.113	1.115	1.116	1.118	1.121	1.123	1.126	1.128	1.131	1.135	1.138	1.141	1.143	1.145
130	1.085	1.091	1.094	1.097	1.099	1.102	1.104	1.107	1.109	1.110	1.112	1.115	1.117	1.120	1.122	1.125	1.129	1.132	1.135	1.137	1.139
135	1.080	1.085	1.088	1.092	1.094	1.097	1.099	1.102	1.104	1.105	1.107	1.110	1.112	1.115	1.117	1.120	1.124	1.127	1.130	1.132	1.134
140	1.075	1.080	1.083	1.087	1.089	1.092	1.094	1.097	1.099	1.100	1.102	1.105	1.107	1.110	1.112	1.115	1.119	1.122	1.125	1.127	1.129
145	1.070	1.075	1.078	1.082	1.084	1.087	1.089	1.092	1.094	1.095	1.097	1.100	1.102	1.105	1.107	1.110	1.114	1.117	1.120	1.122	1.124
150	1.065	1.070	1.073	1.077	1.079	1.082	1.084	1.087	1.089	1.090	1.092	1.095	1.097	1.100	1.102	1.105	1.109	1.112	1.115	1.117	1.119
155	1.059	1.065	1.068	1.071	1.073	1.076	1.078	1.081	1.083	1.084	1.086	1.089	1.091	1.094	1.096	1.099	1.103	1.106	1.109	1.111	1.113
160	1.054	1.059	1.062	1.066	1.068	1.071	1.073	1.076	1.078	1.079	1.081	1.084	1.086	1.089	1.091	1.094	1.098	1.101	1.104	1.106	1.108

The following method of conducting boiler trials has been recommended by the American Society of Mechanical Engineers, and is generally recognized as the standard.

Method of Making a Boiler Test.

A standard method of making a boiler test was adopted by the American Society of Mechanical Engineers, and is published in Vol. VI of the Transactions. This method is complete and should be followed in every case. The method is as follows.

Preliminaries of a Test.

1. *In preparing for* and conducting trials of steam-boilers, the specific object of the proposed trial should be clearly defined and steadily kept in view.

2. *Measure and record the dimensions*, position, etc., of grate and heating surfaces, flues and chimneys, proportion of air-space in the grate surface, kind of draught, natural or forced.

3. *Put the boiler in good condition.*—Have heating surface clean inside and out, grate bars and sides of furnace free from clinkers, dust and ashes removed from back connections leaks in masonry stopped, and all obstructions to draft removed. See that the damper will open to full extent, and that it may be closed when desired. Test for leaks in masonry by firing a little smoky fuel and immediately closing damper. The smoke will then escape through the leaks.

4. *Have an understanding with the parties* in whose interest the test is to be made as to the character of the coal to be used. The coal must be dry, or, if wet, a sample must be dried carefully and a determination of the amount of moisture in the coal made, and the calculation of the results of the test corrected accordingly.

Wherever possible, the test should be made with standard coal of a known quality. For that portion of the country east of the Alleghany Mountains good anthracite egg coal or Cumberland semi-bituminous coal may be taken as the standard for making tests. West of the Alleghany Mountains and east of the Missouri River, Pittsburg lump coal may be used.*

5. *In all important tests* a sample of coal should be selected for chemical analysis.

6. *Establish the correctness of all apparatus* used in the test for weighing and measuring. These are:

a. Scales for weighing coal, ashes and water.

b. Tanks, or water meters for measuring water. Water-meters, as a rule, should only be used as a check on other measurements. For accurate work, the water should be weighed or measured in a tank.

c. Thermometers and pyrometers for taking the temperatures of air, steam, feed-water, waste gases, etc.

d. Pressure-gauges, draught-gauges, etc.

7. *Before beginning a test*, the boiler and chimney should be thoroughly heated to their usual working temperature. If the boiler is new, it should be in continuous use at least a week before testing, so as to dry the mortar thoroughly and heat the walls.

8. Before beginning a test, the boiler and connections should be free from leaks, and all water-connections, including blow and extra feed pipes, should be disconnected or stopped with blank flanges, except the particular pipe through which water is to be fed to the boiler during the trial. In locations where the reliability of the power is so important that an extra feed-pipe must be kept in position, and in general when for any other reason water-pipes other than the feed-pipes cannot be disconnected, such pipes may be drilled so as to leave openings in their lower sides, which should be kept open throughout the test as a means of detecting

---

* These coals are selected because they are almost the only coals which contain the essentials of excellence of quality and adaptability to various kinds of furnaces, grates, boilers and methods of firing and wide distribution and general accessibility in the markets.

leaks, or accidental or unauthorized opening of valves. During the test the blow-off pipe should remain exposed.

If an injector is used, it must receive steam directly from the boiler being tested, and not from a steam-pipe, or from any other boiler.

See that the steam-pipe is so arranged that water of condensation cannot run back into the boiler. If the steam-pipe has such an inclination that the water of condensation from any portion of the steam-pipe system may run back into the boiler, it must be trapped so as to prevent this water getting into the boiler without being measured.

Starting and Stopping a Test.

A test should last at least ten hours of continuous running and twenty-four hours whenever practicable. The conditions of the boiler and furnace in all respects should be, as nearly as possible, the same at the end as at the beginning of the test. The steam.pressure should be the same, the water-level the same, the fire upon the grates should be the same in quantity and condition, and the walls, flues, etc. should be of the same temperature. To secure as near an approximation to exact uniformity as possible in conditions of the fire and in temperatures of the walls and flues, the following method of starting and stopping a test should be adopted :

10. *Standard Method.*—Steam being raised to the working pressure, remove rapidly all the fire from the grate, close the damper, clean the ash-pit, and as quickly as possible start a new fire with weighed wood and coal, noting the time of starting the test and the height of the water-level while the water is in a quiescent state, just before lighting the fire.

At the end of the test remove the whole fire, clean the grates and ash-pit, and note the water-level when the water is in a quiescent state ; record the time of hauling the fire as the end of the test. The water-level should be as nearly as possible the same as at the beginning of the test. If it is not the same a correction should be made by computation, and not by operating pump after test is completed. It will generally be necessary to regulate the discharge of steam from the boiler tested by means of the stop-valve for a time while fires are being hauled at the beginning and end of the test, in order to keep the steam-pressure in the boiler at those times up to the average during the test.

11. *Alternate Method.*—Instead of the Standard Method above described, the following may be employed where local conditions render it necessary :

At the regular time for slicing and cleaning fires have them burned rather low, as is usual before cleaning, and then thoroughly cleaned ; note the amount of coal left on the grate as nearly as it can be estimated ; note the pressure of steam and the height of the water level—which should be at the medium height to be carried throughout the test—at the same time; and note this time as the time of starting the test. Fresh coal, which has been weighed, should now be fired. The ash-pits should be thoroughly cleaned at once after starting. Before the end of the test the fires should be burned low, just as before the start, and the fires cleaned in such a manner as to leave the same amount of fire, and in the same condition, on the grates as at the the start. The water level and steam pressure should be brought to the same point as at the start, and the time of the ending of the test should be noted just before fresh coal is fired.

During the Test.

12. *Keep the Conditions Uniform.*—The boiler should be run continuously, without stopping for meal times or for rise or fall of pressure of steam due to change of demand for steam. The draught being adjusted to the rate of evaporation or combustion desired before the test is begun, it should be retained constant during the test by means of the damper.

If the boiler is not connected to the same steam pipe with

other boilers, an extra outlet for steam with valve in same should be provided, so that in case the pressure should rise to that at which the safety-valve is set, it may be reduced to the desired point by opening the extra outlet, without checking the fires.

If the boiler is connected to a main steam-pipe with other boilers, the safety valve on the boiler being tested should be set a few pounds higher than those of the other boilers, so that in case of a rise in pressure the other boilers may blow off, and the pressure be reduced by closing their dampers, allowing the damper of the boiler being tested to remain open, and firing as usual.

All the conditions should be kept as nearly uniform as possible, such as force of draft, pressure of steam and height of water. The time of cleaning the fires will depend upon the character of the fuel, the rapidity of combustion and the kind of grates. When very good coal is used, and the combustion not too rapid, a ten-hour test may be run without any cleaning of the grates, other than just before the beginning and just before the end of the test. But in case the grates have to be cleaned during the test, the intervals between one cleaning and another should be uniform.

13. *Keeping the Records.*—The coal should be weighed and delivered to the firemen in equal portions, each sufficient for about one hour's run, and a fresh portion should not be delivered until the previous one has all been fired. The time required to consume each portion should be noted, the time being recorded at the instant of firing the first of each new portion. It is desirable that at the same time the amount of water fed into the boiler should be accurately noted and recorded, including the height of the water in the boiler, and the average pressure of steam and temperature of feed during the time. By thus recording the amount of water evaporated by successive portions of coal, the record of the test may be divided into several divisions, if desired, at the end

of the test, to discover the degree of uniformity of combustion, evaporation and economy at different stages of the test.

14. *Priming Tests.*—In all tests in which accuracy of results is important, calorimeter tests should be made of the percentage of moisture in the steam, or of the degree of superheating. At least ten such tests should be made during the trial of the boiler, or so many as to reduce the probable average error to less than one per cent, and the final records of the boiler test corrected according to the average results of the calorimeter tests.

On account of the difficulty of securing accuracy in these tests the greatest care should be taken in the measurements of weights and temperatures. The thermometers should be accurate to within one-tenth of a degree, and the scales on which the water is weighed to within one-hundredth of a pound.

Analyses of Gases.—Measurement of Air-Supply, Etc.

15. In tests for purposes of scientific research, in which the determination of all the variables entering into the test is desired, certain observations should be made which are in general not necessary in tests for commercial purposes. These are the measurement of the air supply, the determination of its contained moisture, the measurement and analysis of the flue-gases, the determination of the amount of heat lost by radiation, of the amount of infiltration of air through the setting, the direct determination by calorimeter experiments of the absolute heating value of the fuel, and (by condensation of all the steam made by the boiler) of the total heat imparted to the water.

The analysis of the flue-gases is an especially valuable method of determining the relative value of different methods of firing, or of different kinds of furnaces. In making these analyses great care should be taken to procure average samples, since the composition is apt to vary at different points of the flue, and the analysis should be intrusted only to a thoroughly competent chemist. who is provided with complete and accurate apparatus.

As the determination of the other variables mentioned above are not likely to be undertaken except by engineers of high scientific attainments, and as apparatus for making them is likely to be improved in the course of scientific research, it is not deemed advisable to include in this code any specific directions for making them.

Record of the Test.

16. A "log" of the test should be kept on properly prepared blanks, containing headings as follows:

Time.	Pressures.			Temperatures.					Fuel.		Feed-water.	
	Barometer.	Steam-gauge.	Draught-gauge.	External Air.	Boiler-room.	Flue.	Feed-water.	Steam.	Time.	Pounds.	Time.	Pounds or c. ft.

Reporting the Trial.

17. The final results should be recorded upon a properly prepared blank, and should include as many of the following items as are adapted for the specific object for which the trial is made. The items marked with a * may be omitted for ordinary trials, but are desirable for comparison with similar data from other sources.

Results of the trials of a..

Boiler at...

To determine...

1. Date of trial................................			
2. Duration of trial............................	hours.		
Dimensions and Proportions.			
Leave space for complete description.			
3. Grate surface...wide...long area...	sq. ft.		
4. Water heating surface..................	sq. ft.		
5. Superheating surface....................	sq. ft.		
6. Ratio of waterheating surface to grate surface.......................................			
Average Pressures.			
7. Steam pressure in boiler by gauge	lbs.		
*8. Absolute steam pressure...............	lbs.		
*9. Atmospheric pressure, per barometer..	in.		
10. Force of draft in inches of water	in.		
Average Temperatures.			
*11. Of external air............................	deg.		
*12. Of fire-room................................	deg.		
*13. Of steam......................................	deg.		
14. Of escaping gases........................	deg.		
15. Of feed water................................	deg.		
Fuel.			
16. Total amount of coal consumed†	lbs.		
17. Moisture in coal	per cent		
18. Dry coal consumed......................	lbs.		
19. Total refuse, dry......pounds=	per cent		
20. Total combustible (dry weight of coal, Item 18, less refuse, Item 19)	lbs.		
*21. Dry coal consumed per hour......	lbs.		
*22. Combustible consumed per hour	lbs.		

* See reference in paragraph preceding table.

† Including equivalent of wood used in lighting fire. 1 pound of wood equals 0.4 pound coal. Not including unburnt coal withdrawn from fire at end of test.

Results of Calorimetric Tests.			
23. Quality of steam, dry steam being taken as unity..			
24. Percentage of moisture in steam	per cent		
25. Number of degrees superheated	deg.		
Water.			
26. Total weight of water pumped into boiler and apparently evaporated*..	lbs.		
27. Water actually evaporated, corrected for quality of steam†	lbs.		
28. Equivalent water evaporated into dry steam from and at 212°F †....	lbs.		
*29. Equivalent total heat derived from fuel in British thermal units †......	B.T.U.		
30. Equivalent water evaporated into dry steam from and at 212° F per hour..................................	lbs		
Economic Evaporation.			
31. Water actually evaporated per pound of dry coal, from actual pressure and temperature †................	lbs.		
32. Equivalent water evaporated per pound of dry coal from and at 212°F †.....................................	lbs.		
33. Equivalent water evaporated per pound of combustible from and at 212°F †................................	lbs.		

* Corrected for inequality of water level and of steam pressure at beginning and end of test.

† The following shows how some of the items in the above table are derived from others :

Item 27 = Item 26 × 23.

Item 28 = Item 27 × Factor of evaporation.

Factor of evaporation = $\frac{H-h}{965.7}$ H and h being respectively the total heat units in steam of the average observed pressure and in water of the average observed temperature of feed, as obtained from tables of the properties of steam and water.

Item 29 = Item 27 × ($H - h$)

Item 31 = Item 27 ÷ Item 18.

Item 32 = Item 28 ÷ Item 18 or = Item 31 × Factor of evaporation.

Item 33 = Item 28 ÷ Item 20 or = Item 32 ÷ (per cent 100 − Item 19).

Items 36 to 38. First term = Item 20 × $\frac{6}{5}$

Items 40 to 42. First term = Item 39 × 0.8698.

Item 43 = Item 29 × 0.00003 or = $\frac{\text{Item } 30}{34\frac{1}{2}}$

Item 45 = $\frac{\text{Difference of Items 43 and 44}}{\text{Item 44}}$

Commercial Evaporation

34. Equivalent water evaporated per pound of dry coal with one sixth refuse, at 70 lbs. gauge-pressure, from temperature of 100° F = Item 33 multiplied by 0.7249........ lbs.

Rate of Combustion.

35. Dry coal actually burned per sq. ft. of grate surface per hour.... lbs.

*36 ⎧ Consumption ⎫ Per sq. ft. of grate surface............... lbs.
*37 ⎨ of dry coal ⎬ Per sq. ft. of water heating surface... lbs.
*38 ⎩ per hour Coal assumed with one sixth refuse. † ⎭ Per sq. ft. of least area for draught lbs.

Rate of evaporation.

39. Water evaporated from and at 212° F per sq. ft. of heating surface per hour.............................. lbs.

*40 ⎧ Water evapor- ⎫ Per sq. ft. of grate surface .... lbs.
*41 ⎨ ated per hour from tempera- ture of 100° F into steam of 70 pounds gauge-pressure† ⎬ Per sq. ft. of water heating surface.. lbs.
*42 ⎩ ⎭ Per square feet of least area for draught .... lbs.

Commercial Horse Power.

43. On basis of thirty pounds of water per hour evaporated from temperature of 100 F into steam of 70 pounds gauge-pressure (= 34¼ lbs. from and at 212°) †...... H.P.

44. Horse-power, builders rating, at ......square feet per horse power.. H.P.

45. Per cent developed above or below rating †............... ....per cent

---

As the foregoing forms of reports will in most cases be unnecessarily full, the following forms for log and reports will be used in ordinary trials of boilers.

TESTING LABORATORY.   Date..............................

  FORM Q.

         LOG OF BOILER TEST NO ....

By...
For ....

Boiler made by...
General Description...
Diameter..............................Length...................................
Dimensions of Dome, Diam...............Length..................
No. of Tubes............Diameter.............Length...............
No. Square Feet Heating Surface......................................
Grate, Length.............Breadth............Surface.............sq. ft.
Draft Area at Bridge....................at Tubes.................sq. ft.
Chimney, Height......................Area.....................sq. ft.

Time.	PRESSURES.			TEMPERATURES.					FUEL.		WATER.	
	Barometer.	Steam Gauge.	Draft Gauge.	External Air.	Boiler Room.	Flue.	Feed Water.	Steam.	Time.	Lbs.	Time.	Lbs.
....	....	....	....	....	....	....	....	....	....	....	....	....
....	....	....	....	....	....	....	....	....	....	....	....	....
....	....	....	....	....	....	....	....	....	....	....	....	....
....	....	....	....	....	....	....	....	....	....	....	....	....
....	....	....	....	....	....	....	....	....	....	....	....	....
....	....	....	....	....	....	....	....	....	....	....	....	....
....	....	....	....	....	....	....	....	....	....	....	....	....
....	....	....	....	....	....	....	....	....	....	....	....	....
....	....	....	....	....	....	....	....	....	....	....	....	....
....	....	....	....	....	....	....	....	....	....	....	....	....
....	....	....	....	....	....	....	....	....	....	....	....	....
....	....	....	....	....	....	....	....	....	....	....	....	....
....	....	....	....	....	....	....	....	....	....	....	....	....
....	....	....	....	....	....	....	....	....	....	....	....	....
....	....	....	....	....	....	....	....	....	....	....	....	....

TESTING LABORATORY. Date..

FORM R.

REPORT OF BOILER TEST NO.......

By ....

For..

Duration of test . .	hrs.	FUEL:	
AVERAGE PRESSURES:		Total Amt. consumed .	lbs.
Barometer . . .	ins.	Moisture in coal . .	p c.
Atmospheric . .	lbs.	Dry coal consumed .	lbs.
Steam gauge . . .	lbs.	Total refuse . . .	lbs.
Absolute steam . .	lbs.	Total combustible . .	lbs.
Draft gauge . . .	ins.	Dry coal per hour .	lbs.
AVERAGE TEMPERATURES		Combustible per hour .	lbs.
External air . . .	deg.	RATE OF COMBUSTION:	
Boiler room . . .	deg.	*Dry coal per hour*	
Flue	deg.	Per sq. ft. Grate . .	lbs.
Feed water . . .	deg.	Per sq. ft. H. S. . .	lbs.
Steam	deg.		

EVAPORATION:

Total water pumped into boiler, lbs. . . . .
Dry steam by calorimeter, per cent . . . .
Actual evaparation corrected for moisture, lbs. . ...
Equivalent evaporation from and at 212°F lbs. . ...
E.E. from and at 212°F per hour, lbs. . . . .
E.E. per lb. of dry coal, lbs. . . . .
E.E. per lb. of combustible, lbs. . . . .

COMMERCIAL EVAPORATION.

E.E. per lb. of dry coal, one sixth refuse, from 100°
Fahn. at 70 lbs. gauge pressure, lbs. . . ..

RATE OF EVAPORATION.

Water evaporated from and at 212° F . . . .
Per sq. ft. of heating surface per hr. . . . .
Per sq. ft. of grate surface per hr. . . . .

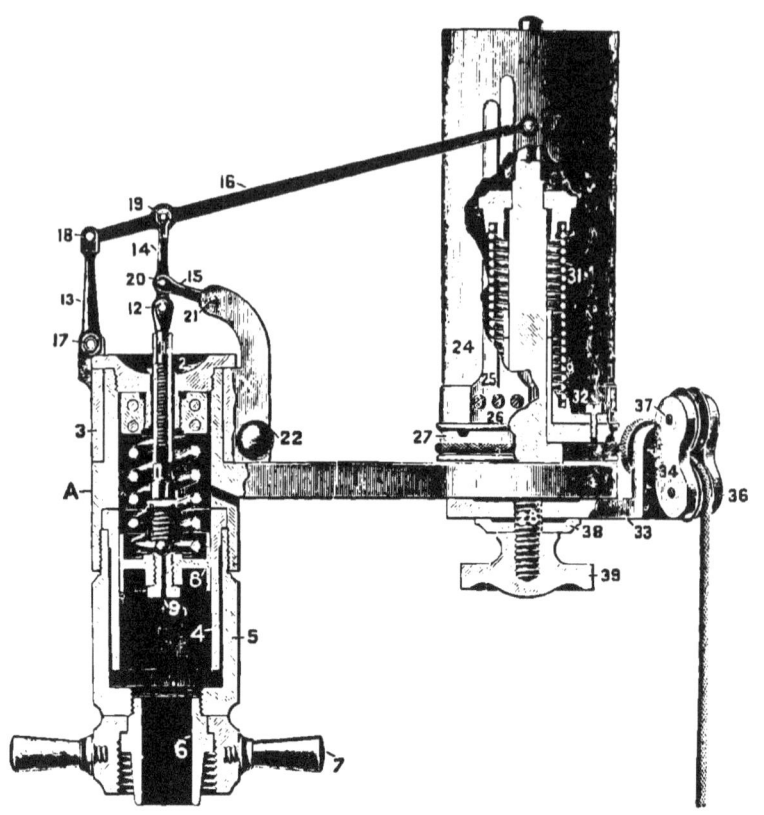

Fig. 19.

Chapter 5.

INDICATORS AND PLANIMETERS.

The steam engine indicator is too well known to need much description. Fig. 19 shows one form of this instrument as manufactured by the Crosby Steam Gauge & Valve Co. and will serve to make clear the general construction of indicators.

The indicator consists in general of the following parts:

1. The cylinder F, which can be attached to the end of the engine cylinder.

2. The piston H, which usually has an area of one-half of a square inch and which should slide easily in the cylinder.

3. The spring N, attached firmly at the upper end to the cap of the cylinder and at the lower end joined to the piston by some form of ball and socket connection, which shall allow the spring to buckle without cramping the piston.

4. The pencil movement K, which shall multiply the motion of the piston in some definite ratio by means of a parallel motion and which is free to turn about the axis of the piston rod.

5. The drum for carrying the paper which receives an oscillating movement from the cross head of the engine, being retracted by a spiral spring.

It would require too much space to attempt to describe all the various forms of indicators which are now on the market

The principle is the same in all, and each experimenter must decide for himself which is best adapted for his particular purpose, and which best satisfies the requirements given in this chapter for a good indicator.

Directions for Care of Indicators.

The indicator is a delicate instrument and must always be properly adjusted and carefully handled, or the results obtained will be very misleading. The pivots and joints of the pencil movement should not be disturbed unless they work loose, but should be frequently oiled with watch or clock oil.

After the indicator has been used the piston and spring should be removed from the cylinder, taken apart, and each piece wiped clean and dry, and slightly oiled before re-assembling.

Before using the indicator the moving parts should be taken from the cylinder and examined to see that they are correctly put together and that there is no lost motion, and a drop or two of cylinder oil should be put on the piston.

The sleeve B and the drum spindle should be occasionally oiled.

Calibration.

The indicator may be most conveniently calibrated by comparison with a standard steam gauge under actual steam pressure. It is of little use to calibrate the springs when cold, by weights or by water pressure, since this method neglects the effect of heat upon the springs.

The following routine may be observed :—

Connect the indicator and the test gauge to a horizontal steam pipe not less than two inches in diameter and so arranged with admission and outlet valves that any desired degree of pressure may be maintained in the pipe.

Allow steam to enter the pipe so that the pressure gradually rises, and at the instant that the pointer on the gauge reaches ten pounds draw a horizontal line on the indicator card by pressing the pencil lightly against the paper and pulling the drum cord by hand.

Allow the pressure to rise another ten pounds and repeat the operation.

Take care that at no time does the pressure rise above the desired point before drawing the line.

After the indicator has been tested to the maximum pressure, tie a knot in the drum cord so that the drum will not return quite to starting point.

This will make the next set of lines distinguishable from the first. Now repeat the experiment beginning with the maximum pressure, allowing the pressure to fall gradually by ten pound intervals, and taking care that it does not get below each desired value until after the line is drawn. Draw the atmospheric line with the steam shut off from the indicator.

Finally with the drum at rest, press pencil against paper and admit steam suddenly to the indicator. The line drawn should be straight and perpendicular to the atmospheric line if it is not, the pencil movement is faulty.

The first set of horizontal lines drawn shows the readings of the indicator spring minus the friction effect of the piston. The second set of lines shows the readings of the spring plus the friction effect. The differences between the two sets will then give twice the friction effect while the average of the two sets will show the real readings of the spring, which may then be compared with the readings of the test gauge.

The following form may be used for log and report of calibration.

TESTING LABORATORY. Date ....
FORM S.

CALIBRATION OF INDICATOR SPRING.

By ....

For ....

Indicator No.................. Made by........................

Scale of Spring.................. Mark..........................

Compared with..

No.	Gauge Reading	True Pressure	Indicator Pressure			Error		Remarks.
			Up	Down	Mean	Total	⅌ Cent	

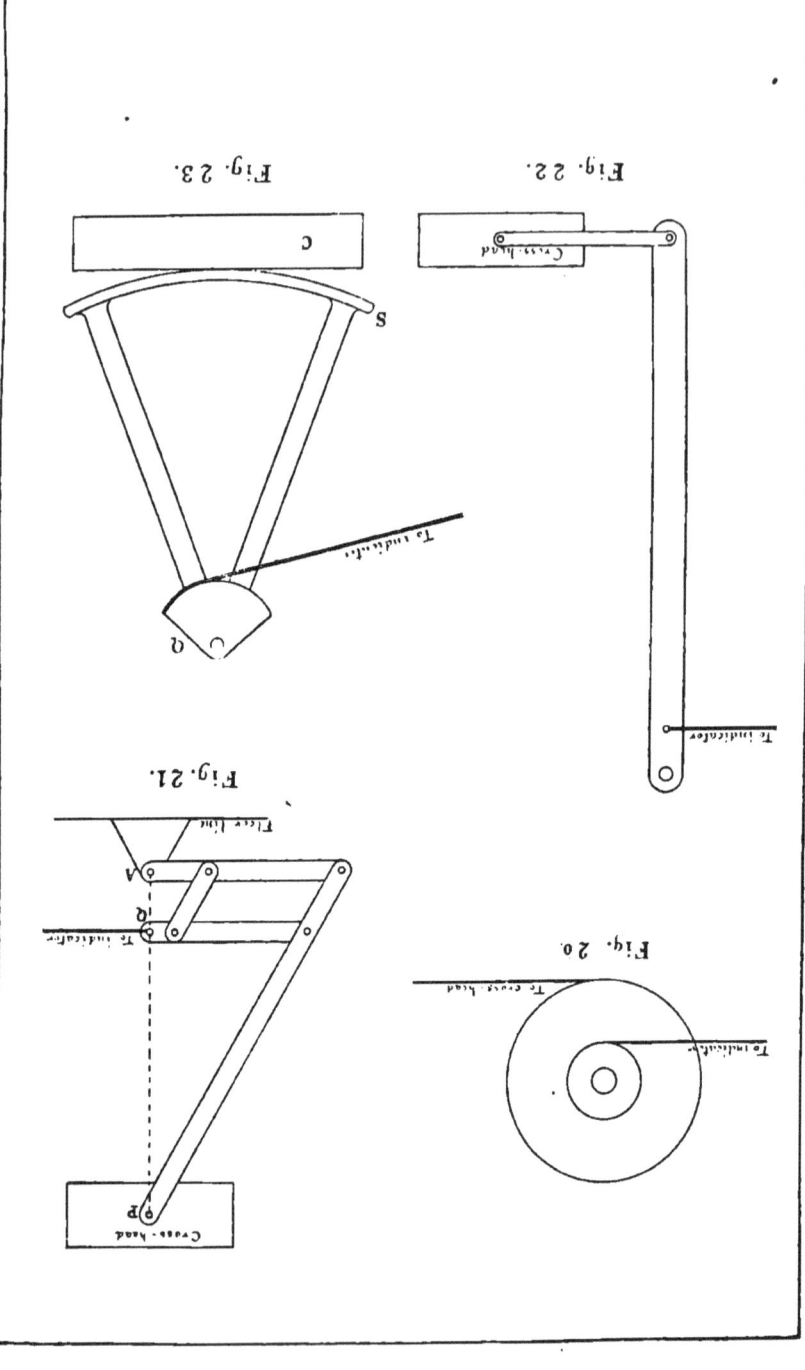

Reducing Motions.

It is always necessary to use some form of reducing motion for connecting the cross-head of the engine with the drum of the indicator. The reducing wheel embodies the old principle of the wheel and axle, the cord from the cross-head leading to the wheel and the cord to the indicator leading from the axle (See Fig. 20). This is a very convenient form of reducing motion, but does not work well at high speeds on account of the inertia of the oscillating parts, while the uneven stretching of the cords introduces considerable error.

One of the best forms of motion is constructed on the principle of the pantograph, the long arm of the pantograph being attached to the cross-head of the engine at P, Fig. 21, and the short arm connected to the indicator cord at Q. The point A being fixed, it is essential that Q shall be in a straight line between A and P and that the ratio

$$\frac{AQ}{AP} = \frac{\text{motion of drum}}{\text{motion of cross-head}}$$

The cord to the indicator must lead off parallel to line of stroke of cross-head.

The swinging pendulum is the simplest and cheapest form of motion, but is usually more or less inaccurate. The form shown in Fig. 22 is fairly accurate if the length of pendulum is great compared with the stroke of the engine. The cord must lead off parallel to line of motion of cross-head and the pendulum must be vertical when the cross-head is in middle position.

Fig. 23 shows a form of swinging pendulum which has been used on engines having horizontal cross-heads and is entirely accurate.

The cord leads off from a quadrant Q in any line tangent to the circle of its edge. The pendulum is moved by a circular segment S rolling on the cross-head C and attached to it by flexible, flat springs which alternately wind on and off the segment.

The cord which leads to the indicator should always be as short as possible and should be of braided linen well stretched. Stretching of the cord may be detected by taking several diagrams at intervals on the same piece of paper. Any difference in the position of the terminal points of the diagrams will show that the cord has changed in length.

Directions for Use.

Attach the indicators one at each end of the cylinder by means of the special cocks which accompany them, first blowing out the cocks to remove any dirt which may have accumulated.

The connections to the cylinder should be as direct as possible and not less than one half inch internal diameter.

See that the cords are of the right length and lead off properly from the reducing motion. Hook on the indicators while the engine is running and see that the drum oscillates evenly so as not to hit the stops at either end.

Unhook cords and put paper on drums, making sure that it is on square and smooth. Adjust pencil points to proper degree of pressure, turn them away from paper and hook up cords again. Turn the indicator cocks half way until steam blows through into the air, then turn them wide open. Put pencil points simultaneously against paper and hold them there until engine has made one revolution (or more if desired).

Shut off steam from indicators and draw the atmospheric lines.

Unhook cords and remove paper from indicators. Examine the diagrams to see if lines are clearly visible and if diagrams are central on paper. If not, make the necessary adjustments before taking more diagrams.

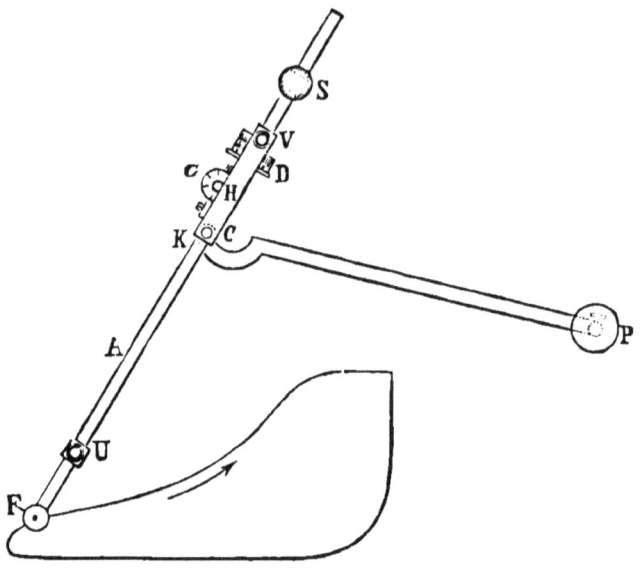

Fig. 24.

Mark on each diagram its number, H or C for head or crank end of cylinder, the time of taking, the number of revolutions per minute and the boiler pressure.

The Polar Planimeter.

As its name implies the planimeter is an instrument for measuring plane areas; it is especially useful in measuring indicator diagrams. The most common form is called the Amsler Polar Planimeter and is shown in Fig. 24 as manufactured by the Crosby Steam Gauge & Valve Co. of Boston.

In its simplest form it consists of two bars pivoted together at K. The end of one bar carries the standing point P which is the pole of the instrument.

The other bar carries the roller wheel D and its vernier from which the readings are taken, while at the outer end of this bar is the tracing point F which is moved by hand around the area to be measured.

Directions for Use.

The planimeter is an even more delicate piece of mechanism than the indicator and *must be handled carefully*.

Provide a flat, even, unglazed surface for the wheel to travel on, such as unglazed, heavy paper or card board. Place the instrument in relation to the diagram about as shown in Fig. 24, so that the point F may move to every part of the outline with freedom.

Place the weight P on the standing point and press the point gently into the paper. Place the tracing point F upon a marked point of the outline and take a reading of the vernier V.

Move the point F around the outline of the diagram in a right-handed direction until it comes back to the starting point and take another reading of the vernier. The difference of the two readings will give the area of the diagram in square inches. If the instrument only reads to ten square inches it is necessary to count the complete revolutions of the wheel for areas exceeding that amount.

When the area is too large to be measured in the ordinary way place the standing point P inside the area and trace the diagram as usual. Watch the roller wheel and note whether on the whole it moves backwards or forwards. If the total rotation is forwards add the difference of the readings of the wheel to the constant of the instrument, which is usually marked on the weight P.

If the rotation is backwards subtract the difference of the readings from the constant.

After using the instrument wipe it carefully with chamois skin and *replace in the box*.

Theory of the Planimeter.

In Fig. 25 let O be the pole of the instrument, P the tracing point, A the joint and W the wheel.

Let $OA = a$
$AP = b$
$AW = c$
$OP = r$

1. Let the point P be moved around the circle whose radius is r and whose area is πr^2. Then will the wheel turn with the same angular velocity as the imaginary wheel W' shown in dotted lines. Let $OW' = x$. The distance moved by the rim of the wheel is then $2\pi x$ while P moves completely around the circle. To find x:

Drop the perpendicular OQ on PA produced; then
$$QW = OW' = x$$
$$\overline{OQ}^2 = r^2 - (b + x - c)^2 = a^2 - (x - c)^2$$
$$r^2 - b^2 - 2bx + 2bc = a^2$$
$$x = \frac{r^2 - a^2 - b^2 + 2bc}{2b}$$
$$2\pi x = \frac{\pi r^2}{b} - \pi \frac{a^2 - 2bc + b^2}{b}$$

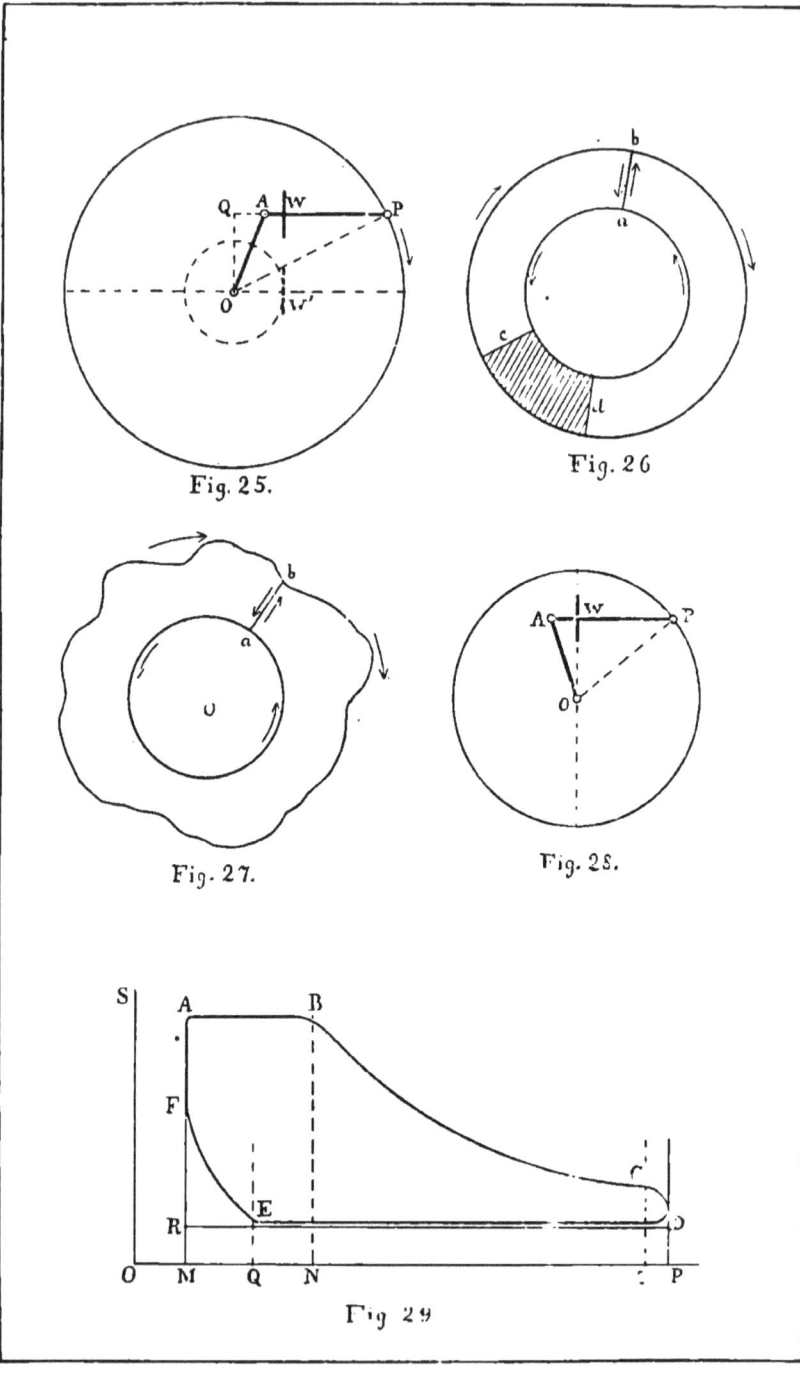

Fig. 25.

Fig. 26

Fig. 27.

Fig. 28.

Fig. 29

That is, the distance moved by rim of wheel, which we will call s is;

$$s = \frac{\text{area}}{b} - \text{a constant}$$

$$\therefore \quad \text{area} = bs + \pi(a^2 - 2bc + b^2)$$

The last term is the area of the circle which would be described if the planimeter were in such a position that $x = 0$ and consequently $s = 0$ (See Fig. 28).

2. Let the area to be measured be a ring or annulus as in Fig. 26. Let outer and inner radii be r and r'.

Then while the tracing point moves from b around the outer circle to b again:

$$s = \frac{\pi r^2}{b} - \text{the constant}$$

Let the wheel move radially in on ba, around the inner circle as shown by the arrows and back on ab to the starting point.

Then will the rolling of the wheel from b to a be neutralized by the rolling from a to b while during the tracing of the inner circle the wheel will turn backwards the amount

$$s' = \frac{\pi r_1^2}{b} - \text{the constant}$$

The net distance turned by the rim of the wheel will therefore be:

$$s - s' = \frac{\pi r^2}{b} - \frac{\pi r_1^2}{b}$$

The area of the ring is: $\pi r^2 - \pi r_1^2 = b(s - s')$ or the reading of the wheel $\times$ b, the constant term having disappeared.

3. Suppose a segment cd of the ring to be traced by the point P. The above statement will also hold true in this case since the rolling at c will be neutralized by that at d while s and s' will be diminished in the same ratio as the area.

But any irregular area can be considered as made up of such segments and its area can be found by multiplying the travel of wheel by b.

It is necessary in this case to have the pole of the instrument outside of the area measured, that the point P may come back to its starting point and that the radial distance moved out may be the same as the radial distance moved in.

4. In case the pole O Fig. 27 is inside the area we may lay off a known circle inside the area and then trace outlines as in Fig. 26, crossing back and forth at ab, and the readings of the wheel will give us the area outside of the circle. But if the circle removed corresponds to the constant area
$$\pi(a^2 - 2bc + b^2)$$
the wheel will not revolve in tracing the circle and it is needless to trace it, or to cross back and forth at ab.

In general therefore we may say that, if the pole of the instrument is outside the area to be measured, the area is equal to the net distance turned by rim of wheel multiplied by the constant b.

That, if the pole is inside the area, to the reading of the wheel must be added the quantity $\pi(a^2 - 2bc + b^2)$ which is a constant for any given planimeter.

For the planimeter as shown in Fig. 25 this constant may be found as follows :

Place the instrument as shown in Fig. 28 and move P in a circle about O. Then W will not revolve as its motion is always parellel to its axis. Using the same notation as before:
$$r^2 = (a^2 - c^2) + (b - c)^2$$
$$= a^2 + b^2 - 2bc$$
$$\therefore \quad \pi r^2 = \pi(a^2 + b^2 - 2bc)$$
and the area of this circle is the constant term sought.

Calibration.

Determine by careful measurement and calculation all the constants of the instrument and see if the constant given is correct.

Measure with the instrument simple known areas of various magnitudes and determine if the vernier reads correctly. Lay out carefully the circle whose radius is $\sqrt{a^2 + b^2 - 2bc}$ and placing the pole of the planimeter at the center, trace the curve and notice if the wheel turns. It is well to mention the fact that the probable errors of observation may be greater than those of the instrument.

The Indicator Diagram.

Fig. 29 represents the ordinary indicator diagram.

AB is the admission line, B the point of cut-off, BC the expansion line, C the point of release, DE the back-pressure line, E the point of compression, EF the compression line, F the point of admission.

RD is the atmospheric line drawn by the indicator. OP is the line of no pressure or vacuum line, drawn parallel to RD and at a distance below it corrresponding to the barometric pressure.

MP is the length of the card and represents the stroke of the engine. OM is a certain per cent of MP and represents to same scale, the clearance (see Heat and Steam p. 40) O is therefore the zero of volume and pressure.

The Indicated Horse Power.

To determine the indicated horse power from an indicator diagram proceed as follows:

Measure the area of the card with the planimeter. Draw lines tangent to the ends of the diagram and perpendicular to the atmospheric line as AM, DP, Fig. 29, thus determining the length of the diagram RD. Divide the area by the length in inches and multiply by the scale of the spring used and this will give the mean effective pressure in pounds per square inch of piston.

Multiply this pressure by the effective area of the piston in square inches, by the length of stroke in feet and by the number of revolutions per minute and divide by 33000, and this will give the indicated horse power of this end of the cylinder. Add to this the horse power as calculated from the diagram from the other end of cylinder and the sum is the total indicated horse power of engine.

In determining the area of piston it is necessary to take into account the area of the cross-section of rod wherever the rod displaces steam.

Indicator cards usually have printed on the back a form for the recording of the various data connected with the test. The following is a convenient form for this purpose.

.............................INDICATOR.

OWNED BY

....

Time.. Date..
Card No.. Scale...
Taken by..
From...end of
.... cylinder
R.P.M..Boiler Press.....................
Work..

ENGINE.	DIAGRAM.
Name	Area...............................
By...................................	Length............................
Diam	M.E.P............................
Stroke.............................	I.H.P.............................
Piston Area.....................	Cut-off...........................
Piston Speed...................	Compression...................
Engine Constant..............	Initial Press...................
Clearance........................	Back Press.....................

Remarks:

The Consumption of Steam.

The indicator diagram shows the amount of steam present in the cylinder at any instant but does not show the water present. The latter can only be determined by actual weighing of the condensed steam from the engine.

To determine the weight of steam present at cut-off, at release and at compression, proceed as follows:

Locate these points as accurately as possible on the diagram as in Fig. 29.

Drop perpendiculars from these points on the vacuum line as BN, CT, EQ. Then will ON, OT, OQ represent to some scale the volumes of steam in the cylinder at these times. To determine the volume, as at ON for instance, multiply the ratio $\frac{ON}{MP}$ by the length of stroke in feet and the area of piston in square feet, and this will give the volume of steam at cut-off in cubic feet. To reduce this to pounds, multiply by the weight of a cubic foot of steam at the indicated pressure BN, as determined from the tables.

A comparison of the amounts of steam shown by the indicator, with the amount actually used as shown by the condenser is an index of the amount of condensation and re-evaporation in the cylinder.

Valve Setting.

Indicators are frequently applied to an engine to see if the valves are properly adjusted, if the work is evenly divided between the two ends of the cylinder and if the governor is working correctly.

A continuous diagram taken while the load is thrown on or off the engine is sometimes of great value in determining the last mentioned point.

There is not space in a work of this kind to describe the various peculiarities of indicator diagrams and the student is referred to works on that subject by Pray, Hemenway and others.

Chapter 6.

TESTING STEAM ENGINES.

The object of making a test of a steam engine is usually to determine its efficiency in terms of the consumption of steam per horse-power per hour, and also if possible to determine the ratio of the net or brake horse-power to the indicated horse power.

Instruments.

The instruments used in a test of this kind have nearly all been described in preceding chapters and may be enumerated as follows :

1. Steam gauge, thermometer and calorimeter to determine the quality of the steam delivered to the engine. These should be located as near the engine as practicable.

2. Indicators, reducing motion, speed counter and planimeter for obtaining diagrams and determining the indicated horse-power and consumption of steam.

The speed counter generally used is a continuous one which simply needs to be read at the beginning and at end of test or at shorter intervals.

3. Some form of absorption brake for determining the net horse-power and insuring a steady load during the run. If the engine tested is driving a factory or electrical machinery, the brake will have to be omitted. In the latter case, mentioned it is usually possible to determine the electrical horse-power instead.

4. Surface condenser, weighing scales and thermometers for determining the quantity and quality of the steam as it leaves the engine.

It is important that all the instruments used in making a test shall be calibrated and their errors noted and allowed for in making the final calculations.

Directions for doing this have been given with the description of each instrument.

The Surface Condenser.

Before using a condenser in an engine test it should be tested for leakage as follows:

Close steam inlet and water outlet and allow all condensed steam to drain from the condenser.

Turn on cold water until the condenser is full and under pressure and notice if any water escapes from the steam outlet.

The following form illustrates the nature of test to determine the efficiency of a surface condenser, and will serve as log and report.

TESTING LABORATORY. Date..........................
FORM T.

REPORT OF CONDENSER TEST.

By..

Condenser made by..
Diameter..............Length..............Capacity..............
No. of Tubes..............Diam..............Length..............
Combined End Area of Tubes..............................
Area of Steam Surface..
Area of Water Surface..

No.					
Duration of test minutes...........					
Barometer reading................					
TEMPERATURES:					
Boiler room					
Entering steam...................					
Condensed steam.................					
Cold condensing water...........					
Hot condensing water............					
WEIGHTS:					
Condensed steam................					
Condensing water...............					
Steam condensed per hour........					
Condensing water per hour.......					
⎰ Steam condensed per sq. ft. ⎱ of steam surface per hr. lbs....					
⎰ Steam condensed per. sq. ft. ⎱ of water surface per hr. lbs.....					
Heat from steam per hr...........					
Heat to water per hr.............					
Velocity of water ft. per minute..					

In case the steam consumption can not be measured in this way it will be necessary to measure the feed water supplied to the boiler, a rather unsatisfactory method at best on account of the danger of leaks and other losses between the feed pump and the engine. Directions for this method will be found under the head of pumping engines.

Directions for Making an Engine Test.

1. See that all the apparatus is in position and in good working order, and that every observer is in his place. Assign one man to the position of time-keeper, whose duty it shall be to give signals for starting and stopping the test by means of a gong or whistle and to note the time.

2. Make a preliminary run of ten minutes to see that the signals are understood, that each observer knows what he is to do and that all the apparatus is working satisfactorily.

3. Make a continuous run as long as may be desired (thirty minutes is long enough unless the load is variable). Have indicator cards taken every five minutes and the observations of calorimeter, thermometers and brake made at the same intervals. The condensed steam can be weighed most accurately by allowing it to run through a short piece of hose until the signal for starting is given when it can instantly be turned into the barrel on the weighing scales.

At the signal for stopping the test the hose can be instantly removed. In long runs it is necessary to have two scales and two barrels, emptying one while the other is being filled.

4. Measure the necessary dimensions of the engine and its connections and note them on the form provided for this purpose.

The accompanying forms will explain the details of the log and report.

TESTING LABORATORY.　　　　Date..............................
FORM U.

LOG OF ENGINE TEST, NO............

By...

For...

Engine made by...

Diameter of Cylinder...............inches.　Stroke........... feet

Piston Area, Head........................　Crank.........sq. in.

Piston Displacement, Head...............　Crank.........cu. ft.

Per Cent Clearance, Head...............　Crank.........

Engine H. P. Constant, Head...........　Crank.........

Observed	Begin'ing	End	Results
Time			Duration of test, min
Engine counter			Total Revs. of Engine
Brake Counter			Total Revs. of Brake
Weight of barrel			Weight of steam used

TEMPERATURES	PRESSURES
Entering steam............................	Barometer..............................
Exhaust steam..........................	Boiler.................................
Engine room.............................	Steam pipe.............................

Per Cent of Dry Steam by Calorimeter............................

Load on Brake.... ....

Numbers of Indicator Cards taken........ ....

Calculated from above :

Revolutions per minute of Engine. .... of Brake...........

Steam used per minute..............................lbs.

Mean eff. pressure, Head ....Crank...............

TESTING LABORATORY. Date..................................
FORM V.

REPORT OF ENGINE TEST, NO.........

By..

For...

Horse Power	Head	Crank	Actual Water Used.
Engine constant	....	....	Water per min................
Revs. per minute	....	....	
Mean eff. pressure	....	....	Water per hour...............
Ind. horse power	....	....	Water per rev.$=w$.........
Total ind. horse power	....		Water per $\}$ ....
Brake horse power	....		IHP per hr. $\}$
Friction horse power	....		Dry steam per $\}$ ....
			IHP per hr. $\}$

	Steam Shown by Indicator					
See page 79	Head End			Crank End		
Indicated pressure	....	....	....	....	....	....
Barometer pressure	....	....	....	....	....	....
Absolute pressure	....	....	....	....	....	....
Weight cu. ft. steam	....	....	....	....	....	....
Per cent volume	....	....	....	....	....	....
Volume of cylinder	....	....	....	....	....	....
Weight of steam	....	....	....	....	....	....
Weight, crank end	....	....	....	Mixture in cylinder per rev.		
	x	y	z			
Total weight per rev.	....	....	....	$=w+z=$		

Checked by...

TESTING LABORATORY.
FORM W.

Date...

REPORT OF ENGINE TEST, NO.............(Continued)

By ....

For...

Steam at Cut-off	Steam at Release
x per revolution	y per revolution..........................
$w + z$ per revolution...............	$w + z$ per revolution...............
Per cent steam.......................	Per cent steam.......................
Re-evaporation	Steam Used
y per revolution......................	y per revolution.....................
$\dfrac{x \text{ per revolution}......................}{y - x \text{ per revolution}...............}$	$\dfrac{z \text{ per revolution.......................}}{y - z \text{ per revolution................}}$
Revs. per hour........................	
Indicated HP.........................	Indicated steam $\Big\}$ .... per IHP per hr.
Re-evaporation $\Big\}$ .... per IHP per hr.	Actual dry steam $\Big\}$ .... per IHP per hr.

Remarks :

Pumping Engine.

The foregoing general instructions do not apply to pumping engines.

A standard method of testing this class of engines has been recommended by the American Society of Mechanical Engineers, and is as follows :

(1) Test of Feed Water Temperatures.

The plant is subjected to a preliminary run, under the conditions determined upon for the test, for a period of three hours, or such a time as is necessary to find the temperature of the feed-water (or the several temperatures, if there is more than one supply) for use in the calculation of the duty. During this test observations of the temperature are made every fifteen minutes. Frequent observations are also made of the speed, length of stroke, indication of water-pressure gauges and other instruments, so as to have a record of the general condition under which this test is made.

Directions for obtaining Feed-water Temperatures.—When the feed-water is all supplied by one feeding instrument, the temperature to be found is that of the water in the feed-pipe near the point where it enters the boiler. If the water is fed by an injector, this temperature is to be corrected for the heat added to the water by the injector, and for this purpose the temperature of the water entering and of that leaving the injector are both observed. If the water does not pass through a heater on its way to the boiler (that is, that form of heater which depends upon the rejected heat of the engine such as that contained in the exhaust steam either of the main cylinder or of the auxiliary pumps), it is sufficient for practical purposes, to take the temperature of the water at the source of supply, whether the feeding instrument is a pump or an injector.

When there are two independent sources of feed-water supply, one the main supply from the hot-well, or from some other source, and the other an auxiliary supply derived from the water condensed in the jackets of the main engine and in the live-steam re-heater, if one be used, they are to be treated independently. The remarks already made apply to the first or main supply. The temperature of the auxiliary supply, if carried by an independent pipe either direct to the boiler or to the main feed-pipe near the boiler, is to be taken at convenient points in the independent pipe.

When a separator is used in the main steam pipe, arranged so as to discharge the entrained water back in to the boiler by gravity, no account need be made of the temperature of the water thus returned. Should it discharge either into the atmosphere to waste, to the hot well or to the jacket tank, its temperature is to be determined at the point where the water leaves the separator before its pressure is reduced.

When a separator is used, and it drains by gravity into the jacket-tank, this tank being subjected to boiler pressure, the temperature of the separator-water and jacket-water are each to be taken before their entrance to the tank.

Should there be any other independent supply of water, the temperature of that is also to be taken on this preliminary test.

Directions for Measurment of Feed-water.—As soon as the feed-water temperatures have been obtained the engine is stopped, and the necessary apparatus arranged for determining the weight of the feed water consumed, or of the various supplies of feed water if there is more than one.

In order that the main supply of feed-water may be measured, it will generally be found desirable to draw it from the cold-water service main. The best form of apparatus for weighing the water consists of two tanks one of which rests upon a platform-scale supported by staging, while the other is placed underneath. The water is drawn from the service main into the upper tank, where it is weighed, and it is then emptied into the lower tank. The lower tank serves as a reservoir, and to the suction-pipe of the feeding apparatus is connected.

The jacket water may be measured by using a pair of small barrels, one being filled while the other is being weighed and emptied. This water, after being measured, may be thrown away, the loss being made up by the main feed-pump. To prevent evaporation from the water, and consequent loss on account of its highly heated condition, each barrel should be partially filled with cold water previous to using it for collecting the jacket-water, and the weight of this water treated as tare.

When the jacket-water drains back by gravity to the boiler waste of live steam during the weighing should be prevented by providing a small vertical chamber and conducting the water into this receptacle before its escape. A glass water-gauge is attached, so as to show the height of water inside the chamber, and this serves as a guide in regulating the discharge-valve.

When the jacket water is returned to the boiler by means of a pump, the discharge-valve should be throttled during the test, so that the pump may work against its usual pressure, that is, the boiler-pressure as nearly as may be, a gauge being attached to the discharge-pipe for this purpose.

When a separator is used and the entrained water discharges either to waste, to the hot-well or to the jacket tank, the weight of this water is to be determined, the water being drawn into barrels in the manner pointed out for measuring the jacket-water. Except in the case where the separator discharges into the jacket-tank, the entrained water thus found is treated in the calculations, in the same manner as moisture shown by the calorimeter-test. When it discharges into the jacket tank, its weight is simply subtracted from the total weight of water fed, and allowance made for heat of this water lost by radiation between separator and tank.

When the jackets are drained by a trap, and the condensed water goes either to waste or to the hot-well, the determination of the quantity used is not necessary to the main object of the duty-trial, because the main feed-pump in such cases supplies all the feed-water. For the sake of having complete data, however, it is desirable that this water be measured, whatever the use to which it is applied.

Should live steam be used for reheating the steam in the intermediate receiver, it is desirable to separate this from the jacket-steam if it drain into the same tank and measure it independently. This, likewise, is not essential to the main object of the duty trial, though useful for purposes of information.

The remarks as to the manner of preventing losses of live steam and of evaporation, in the measurement of jacket-water apply to the measurement of any other hot water under pressure, which may be used for feed-water.

Should there be any other independent supply of water to the boiler besides those named, its quantity is to be determined independently, apparatus for all these measurements being set up during the interval between the preliminary run and the main trial, when the plant is idle.

(2) The Main Duty-trial.

The duty-trial is here assumed to apply to a complete plant embracing a test of the performance of the boiler as well as that of the engine. The test of the two will go on simultaneously after both are started, but the boiler test will begin a short time in advance of the commencement of the engine-test and continue a short time after the engine-test is finished. The mode of precedure is as follows:

The plant having been worked for a suitable time under normal conditions, the fire is burned down to a low point and the engine brought to rest. The fire remaining on the grate is then quickly hauled, the furnace cleaned, and the refuse withdrawn from the ash-pit. The boiler test is now started, and this test is made in accordance with the rules for a standard method recommended by the Committee on Boiler Tests of the American Society of Mechanical Engineers. This method briefly described, consists in starting the test with a new fire lighted with wood, the boiler having previously been heated to its normal working degree; operating the boiler in accordance with the conditions determined upon; weighing coal, ashes and feed-water; observing the draught, temperatures of feed-water and escaping gases, and such other data as may be incidentally desired; determining the quantity of moisture in the coal and in the steam; and at the close of the test hauling the fire, and deducting from the weight of coal fired whatever unburned coal is contained in the refuse withdrawn from the furnace, the quantity of water in the boiler and the steam-pressure being the same as at the time of lighting the fire at the beginning of the test.

Previous to the close of the test it is desirable that the fire should be burned down to a low point, so that the unburned coal withdrawn may be in a nearly consumed state. The temperature of the feed-water is observed at the point where the water leaves the engine heater, if this be used or at the point where it enters the flue-heater, if that apparatus be employed. Where an injector is used for supplying the water a deduction is to be made in either case for the increased temperature of the water derived from the steam which it consumes.

As soon after the beginning of the boiler-test as practicable the engine is started and preparations are made for the beginning of the engine-test. The formal commencement of this test is delayed till the plant is again in normal working condition, which should not be over one hour after the time of lighting the fire. When the time for commencement arrives the feed-water is momentarily shut off, and the water in the lower tank is brought to a mark. Observations are then made of the number of tanks of water thus far supplied, the height of water in the gauge-glass of the boiler, the indication of the counter on the engine, and the time of day; after which the supply of feed-water is renewed and the regular observations of the test, including the measurement of the auxiliary supplies of feed-water, are commenced. The engine-test is to continue at least ten hours. At its expiration the feed-pump is again momentarily stopped, care having been taken to have the water slightly higher than at the start, and the water in the lower tank is brought to the mark. When the water in the gauge-glass has settled to the point which it occupied at the beginning, the time of day and the indication of the counter are observed, together with the number of tanks of water thus far supplied, and the engine test is held to be finished. The engine continues to run after this time till the fire reaches a condition for hauling, and completing the boiler-test. It is then stopped and the final observations relating to the boiler-test are taken.

The observations to be made and the data obtained for the purposes of the engine test, or duty-trial proper, embrace the weight of feed-water supplied by the main feeding apparatus, that of the water drained from the jackets, and any other water which is ordinarily supplied to the boiler, determined in the manner pointed out. They also embrace the number of hours duration, and number of single strokes of the pump during the test; and, in direct acting engines, the length of the stroke, together with the indications of the gauges attached to the force and suction mains, and indicator-diagram from the steam cylinders. It is desirable that pump-diagrams also be obtained.

Observations of the length of stroke, in the case of direct-acting engines, should be made every five minutes; observations of the water-pressure gauges every fifteen minutes; observations of the remaining instruments—such as steam-gauge, vacuum-gauge, thermometer in pump-well, thermometer in feed-pipe; thermometer showing temperature of engine-room, boiler-room and outside air; thermometer in flue, thermometer in steam-pipe, if the boiler has steam-heating surface, barometer and other instruments which may be used—every half-hour. Indicator-diagrams should be taken every half-hour.

When the duty-trial embraces simply a test of the engine apart from the boiler, the course of procedure will be the same as that described, excepting that the fires will not be hauled, and the special observations relating to the performance of the boiler will not be taken.

Directions regarding Arrangement and Use of Instruments and other Provisions for the Test.—The gauge attached to the force-main is liable to a considerable amount of fluctuation unless the gauge-cock is nearly closed. The practice of choking the cock is objectionable. The difficulty may be satisfactorily overcome, and a nearly steady indication secured with cock wide open, if a small reservoir having an air-chamber is interposed between the gauge and the force-main. By means of a gauge-glass on the side of the chamber and an air-valve, the average water-level may be adjusted to the height of the center of the gauge, and correction for this element of variation is avoided. If not thus adjusted, the reading is to be referred to the level shown, whatever this may be.

To determine the length of stroke in the case of direct-acting engines, a scale should be securely fastened to the frame which connects the steam and water cylinders in a position parallel to the piston-rod, and a pointer attached to the rod as as to move back and forth over the graduations on the scale. The marks on the scale, which the pointer reaches at the two ends of the stroke, are thus readily observed, and the distance moved over computed. If the length of the stroke can be determined by the use of some form of registering apparatus, such a method of measurement is preferred. The personal errors in observing the exact scale-marks, which are liable to creep in, may thereby be avoided.

The form of calorimeter to be used for testing the quality of the steam is left to the decision of the person who conducts the trial. It is preferred that some form of continuous calorimeter be used, which acts directly on the moisture tested. If either the superheating calorimeter or the wire-drawing instrument be employed, the steam which it discharges is to be measured either by numerous short trials, made by condensing it in a barrel of water previously weighed, thereby obtaining the rate by which it is discharged, or by passing it through a surface-condenser of some simple construction, and measuring the whole quantity consumed. When neither of these instruments is at hand, and dependence must be placed upon the barrel calorimeter, scales should be used which are sensitive to a change in weight of a small fraction of a pound, and thermometers which may be read to tenths of a degree. The pipe which supplies the calorimeter should be thoroughly warmed and drained just previous to each test. In making the calculations the specific heat of the material of the barrel or tank should be taken into account whether this be of metal or of wood.

If the steam is superheated, or if the boiler is provided with steam-heating surface, the temperature of the steam is to be taken by means of a high-grade thermometer resting in a cup holding oil or mercury, which is screwed into the steam pipe so as to be surrounded by the current of steam. The temperature of the feed-water is preferably taken by means of a cup screwed into the feed-pipe in the same manner.

Indicator-pipes and connections used for the water-cylinders should be of ample size, and, so far as possible, free from bends. Three-quarter-inch pipes are preferred, and the indicators should be attached one at each end of the cylinder. It should be remembered that indicator-springs which are correct under steam heat are erroneous when used for cold water. When such springs are used, the actual scale should be determined, if calculations are made of the indicated work done in the water-cylinders. The scale of steam-springs should be determined by a comparison, under steam-pressure with an accurate steam-gauge at the time of the trial, and that of water-springs by cold dead-weight test.

The accuracy of all the gauges should be carefully verified by comparison with a reliable mercury column. Similar verification should be made of the thermometers, and if no standard is at hand, they should be tested in boiling water and melting ice.

To avoid errors in conducting the test, due to leakage of stop-valves either on the steam-pipes, feed-water pipes or blow-off pipes all these pipes not concerned in the operation of the plant under test should be disconnected.

(3) Leakage-test of Pump.

As soon as practicable after the completion of the main trial (or at some time immediately preceding the trial) the engine is brought to rest and the rate determined at which leakage takes place through the plunger and valves of the pump, when these are subjected to the full pressure of the force-main.

The leakage of the plunger is most satisfactorily determined by making the test with the cylinder-head removed. A wide board or plank may be temporarily bolted to the lower part of the end of the cylinder, so as to hold back the water in the manner of a dam, and an opening made in the temporary head thus provided for the reception of an overflow pipe. The plunger is blocked at some intermediate point in the stroke (or if this position is not practicable, at the end of the stroke), and the water from the force-main is admitted at full pressure behind it. The leakage escapes through the overflow pipe, and it is collected in barrels and measured.

Should the escape of the water into the engine-room be objectionable, a spout may be constructed to carry it out of the building. Where the leakage is too great to be readily measured in barrels, or where other objections arise, resort may be had to weir or orifice measurement, the weir or orifice taking the place of the overflow-pipe in the wooden head. The apparatus may be constructed, if desired, in a somewhat rude manner, and yet be sufficiently accurate for practical requirements. The test should be made, if possible, with the plunger in various positions.

In the case of a pump so planned that it is difficult to remove the cylinder-head, it may be desirable to take the leakage from one of the openings which are provided for the inspection of the suction-valves the head being allowed to remain in place.

It is here assumed that there is a practical absence of valve-leakage a condition of things which ought to be attained in all well-constructed pumps. Examination for such leakage should be made first of all, and if it occurs and it is found to be due to disordered valves, it should be remiedied before making the plunger-test. Leakage of the discharge valves will be shown by water passing down into the empty cylinder at either end when they are under pressure. Leakage of the suction valves will be shown by the disapperance of water which covers them.

If valve-leakage is found which cannot be remedied, the quantity of water thus lost should also be tested. The determination of the quantity which leaks through the suction-valves where there is no gate in the suction-pipe must be made by indirect means. One method is to measure the amount of water required to maintain a certain pressure in the pump cylinder when this is introduced through a pipe temporarily erected, no water being allowed to enter through the discharge-valves of the pump.

The exact methods to be followed in any particular case in determining leakage, must be left to the judgment and ingenuity of the person conducting the test.

(4) Table of Data and Results.

In order that uniformity may be secured, it is suggested that the data and results, worked out in accordance with the standard method, be tabulated in the manner indicated in the following scheme.

DUTY-TRIAL OF ENGINE.

Dimensions.

1. Number of steam-cylinders..........................
2. Diameter of steam-cylinders .... ins.
3. Diam. of piston-rods of steam cylinders.......... ins.
4. Nominal stroke of steam-pistons.................... ft.
5. Number of water-plungers............................
6. Diameter of plungers................................... ins.
7. Diam. of piston-rods of water cylinders........... ins.
8. Nominal stroke of plungers........................... ft.
9. Net area of plungers................................... sq. in.
10. Net area of steam pistons............................ sq. in.
11. Average length of stroke of steam-pistons during trial.. ft.
12. Average length of stroke of plungers during trial ft.
   (Give also complete description of plant.)

Temperatures.

13. Temperature of water in pump-well................ degs.
14. Temperature of water supplied to boiler by main feed-pump....................................... degs.
15. Temperature of water supplied to boiler from various other sources................................ degs.

Feed-water.

16. Weight of water supplied to boiler by main feed-pump.. lbs.
17. Weight of water supplied to boiler from various other sources... lbs.

18. Total weight of feed-water supplied from all sources.. lbs.

Pressures.

19. Boiler-pressure indicated by gauge................ lbs.
20. Pressure indicated by gauge on force-main...... lbs.
21. Vacuum indicated by gauge on suction-main.... ins.
22. Pressure corresponding to vacuum given in preceding line... lbs.
23. Vertical distance between the centers of the two gauges... ins.
24. Pressure equivalent to distance between the two gauges... lbs.

Miscellaneous Data.

25. Duration of trial.................................... hrs.
26. Total number of single strokes during trial......
27. Percentage of moisture in steam supplied to engine, or number of degrees of superheating % or deg.
28. Total leakage of pump during trial, determined from results of leakage-test...................... lbs.
29. Mean effective pressure, measured from diagrams taken from steam-cylinders...................... M. E. P.

Principal Results.

30. Duty... ft.-lbs.
31. Percentage of leakage............................... %
32. Capacity... gals.
33. Percentage of total frictions....................... %

Additional Results.*

34. Number of double strokes of steam-piston per minute..
35. Indicated horse-power developed by the various steam-cylinders.................................... I. H. P.
36. Feed-water consumed by the plant per hr........ lbs.
37. Feed-water consumed by the plant per indicated horse-power per hour corrected for moisture in steam.. lbs.

---

* These are not necessary to the main object, but it is desirable to give them.

38. Number of heat-units consumed per indicated
horse-power per hour............................... B.T.U.
39. Number of heat-units consumed per indicated
horse-power per minute........................... B.T.U.
40. Steam accounted for by indicator at cut-off and
release in the various steam-cylinders......... lbs.
41. Proportion which steam accounted for by indicator bears to the feed-water consumption...

Sample Diagrams taken from Steam-cylinders.

(Also, if possible, full measurements of the diagrams, embracing pressures at the initial point, cut-off, release and compression; also back-pressure, and the proportions of the stroke completed at the various points noted.)

42. Number of double strokes of pump per minute
43. Mean effective pressure, measured from pump
diagrams.. M.E.P.
44. Indicated horse-power exerted in pump cylinders I.H.P.

Sample Diagrams taken from Pump-cylinders.

....
....
....

If a boiler trial is made in connection with the engine trial the same method is recommended as that given in Chapter 4.

The following forms for log and report are given for use in making a test of a boiler feed pump and need no additional explanation.

TESTING LABORATORY.　　　　Date..........................

FORM X.

LOG OF PUMP TEST, NO............ /

By..

For...

Pump made by...

Used for..

Dimensions.	Steam End.	Water End.
Diameter of piston, inches . .	....	....
Area of piston, sq. inches	....	....
Stroke in feet . . .	....	....
Displacement in cubic feet	....	....
Per cent clearance . . .	....	....

Diameter in inches of steam pipe...................................

Exhaust pipe............ Suction............ Feed............

Piston rod...............

Observed.	Begin'ing	End.		Results.
Time .	....	......	......	Duration of test min
Counter .	....	......	......	Total No. strokes
Water in tank	....	......	......	Lbs. water delivered
Water in boiler .	....	......	......	Inches in boiler
Difference of level, ft.	....	......	......	Average lift in feet
Weight of barrel, lbs.	....	......	. ...	Total steam used

Pressures: Barometer............ Boiler Gauge............

Calculated from above:

Strokes per minute of Pump.................................

Steam used per minute ....lbs.

Water delivered per stroke ....lbs.

M.E.P. Steam End............... Water End...............

TESTING LABORATORY.
FORM Y.

Date..

REPORT OF PUMP TEST, NO.........

By..

For..

Work.			
Water per stroke, cu. ft............		Water per stroke, lbs.	
Slip per stroke cu. ft.		Lift in feet	
Per cent slip		Work of lifting	
Boiler press. lbs. sq. ft............		Pressure work	
Pressure work per stroke } ft. lbs.		Total work per stroke } ft. lbs.	
Horse Power.	Steam End.	Water End.	Net.
Mean eff. pressure			
Area piston, sq. ins.			
Stroke in feet			
Work per stroke, ft. lbs.			
Strokes per minute			
Horse Power			
Steam per minute, lbs.			
Steam per hour, lbs.			
Steam per HP per hr.			

Per cent of power used in :

Pump friction............ Pipe friction......... Work.........

Checked by..

THE PROPERTIES OF SATURATED STEAM.

Pressure in lbs. per sq. inch above the atmosphere.	Temperature of steam in degrs. Fahrenheit.	Heat above 32° F. in water at boiling point.	External work in heat units.	T'l heat above 32° Fahr. in steam.	Internal work of evaporati'n in heat units.	Latent heat of evaporation in heat units	Total internal work above 32° in heat units.	Weight of one cubic foot of steam in pounds.	Volume of 1 lb. in cubic feet.
—14	90	.....	...	1109	.....	....	in	......	......
—13	121	99	62	1118	967	1029	1070	0.006	172.0
—12	138	106	65	1124	943	1018	as	0.008	117.5
—11	150	118	67	1127	942	1009	taken	0.011	89.6
—10	160	128	67	1130	935	1002	be	.014	72.6
— 9	168	136	67	1133	925	993	may practice.	.016	61.2
— 8	175	143	68	1134	923	991		.019	52.9
— 7	181	150	68	1137	918	987		.021	46.7
— 6	187	156	69	1138	913	982	these	.024	41.8
— 5	192	161	69	1140	909	979	All	.026	37.8
— 4	196	165	70	1141	906	976		.029	34.6
— 3	201	170	70	1143	903	973		.031	31.8
— 2	205	174	71	1144	899	970		.034	29.5
— 1	209	178	71	1145	896	967		.036	27.6
0	212	181	72	1146	893	965	1074	.038	26.3
1	215	184	72	1147	890	962	1074	.041	24.3
2	219	188	72	1148	888	960	1076	.043	23.0
3	222	191	73	1149	887	958	1078	.046	21.8
4	225	194	73	1150	885	956	1079	.048	20.7
5	227	196	73	1151	882	953	1079	.050	19.7
6	230	199	74	1152	879	951	1079	.053	18.8
7	233	202	74	1152	877	950	1079	.055	18.0
8	235	204	74	1153	876	948	1079	.058	17.2
9	237	206	74	1154	873	947	1080	.060	16.6
10	239	208	74	1154	872	945	1080	.062	16.0
11	242	211	75	1155	869	944	1080	.065	15.4
12	244	213	75	1156	867	942	1080	.067	14.9
13	246	215	75	1156	866	941	1081	.070	14.4
14	248	217	75	1157	864	939	1081	.072	13.9
15	250	220	75	1158	863	938	1083	.074	13.4
16	252	222	75	1158	862	937	1083	.076	13.0
17	254	224	76	1159	859	935	1084	.079	12.7
18	256	226	76	1159	858	934	1084	.081	12.3
19	257	227	76	1160	857	933	1084	.083	12.0
20	259	229	76	1160	856	932	1085	.086	11.6
22	262	232	76	1161	853	929	1085	.090	11.0
24	266	236	77	1162	850	927	1086	.095	10.6
26	269	239	77	1163	848	925	1087	.099	10.0
28	272	242	77	1164	846	923	1088	.104	9.6
30	274	244	77	1165	844	921	1088	.109	9.2
35	281	251	78	1167	838	916	1089	.120	8.3
40	287	257	78	1169	834	912	1091	.131	7.6
45	293	263	78	1171	830	908	1093	.142	7.0
50	298	268	79	1172	825	904	1093	.154	6.5

THE PROPERTIES OF SATURATED STEAM.

Pressure in lbs per sq. inch above the atmosphere.	Temperature of steam in degrees Fahrenheit.	Heat above 32° F. in water at boiling point.	External work in heat units.	T'l heat above 32° Fahr. in steam.	Internal work of evaporation in heat units.	Latent heat of evaporation in heat units.	Total internal work above 32° in heat units.	Weight of 1 cubic foot of steam in pounds.	Volume of 1 lb. in cubic feet.
55	303	273	79	1174	822	901	1095	.165	6.1
60	307	278	79	1175	818	897	1096	.176	5.7
65	312	282	80	1176	814	894	1097	.187	5.3
70	316	287	80	1178	811	891	1098	.198	5.0
75	320	291	80	1179	808	888	1099	.209	4.8
80	324	294	80	1180	806	886	1100	.220	4.5
85	328	298	81	1181	802	883	1100	.231	4.3
90	331	301	81	1182	800	881	1101	.241	4.1
95	334	305	81	1183	798	878	1101	.252	4.0
100	338	308	81	1184	795	876	1102	.263	3.8
105	341	311	82	1185	792	874	1103	.274	3.6
110	344	315	82	1186	789	871	1104	.284	3.5
115	347	318	82	1187	787	869	1105	.295	3.4
120	350	321	82	1188	785	867	1106	.306	3.3
125	353	324	82	1189	783	865	1107	.316	3.2
130	355	327	82	1190	781	863	1108	.327	3.1
135	358	329	82	1191	779	861	1108	.338	3.0
140	361	331	83	1191	777	860	1109	.348	2.9
145	363	334	83	1192	775	858	1109	.359	2.8
150	366	337	83	1193	773	856	1110	.369	2.7
155	368	340	83	1194	771	854	1111	.380	2.6
160	371	341	83	1194	770	853	1111	.390	2.6
165	373	344	83	1195	768	851	1112	.400	2.5
170	375	347	84	1196	765	849	1112	.412	2.4
175	377	348	84	1196	764	848	1113	.422	2.4
180	380	351	84	1197	762	846	1113	.433	2.3
185	382	353	84	1198	761	845	1114	.443	2.3
195	386	357	84	1199	758	842	1115	.463	2.2
205	390	361	85	1200	754	839	1115	.484	2.1
215	394	365	85	1201	751	836	1116	.505	2.0
225	397	368	85	1202	749	834	1117	.525	1.9
235	401	373	85	1204	746	831	1119	.546	1.8
245	404	376	85	1205	744	829	1120	.567	1.8
255	408	380	85	1206	741	826	1121	.587	1.7
265	411	383	85	1207	739	824	1122	.608	1.6
275	414	386	85	1208	737	822	1123	.627	1.6
285	417	389	86	1209	734	820	1123	.649	1.5
335	430	392	86	1213	725	811	1127	.750	1.3
385	445	417	86	1217	714	800	1131	.850	1.2
* *	* *	* *	* *	* *	* *	* *	* *	* *	† †
435	457	428	87	1220	705	792	1133	.950	1.05
485	467	440	87	1224	697	784	1137	1.049	0.95
585	487	460	87	1230	683	770	1143	1.245	0.80
685	504	477	88	1235	670	758	1147	1.439	0.69
785	519	493	88	1240	659	747	1152	1.632	0.61
885	534	507	88	1244	649	737	1156	1.823	0.55
985	516	520	88	1248	640	728	1160	2.014	0.50

Values below * * are computed and not experimental.
NOTE.—For all values of Total Internal work below the atmosphere 1070 heat units may be taken. All decimal parts of heat units have been neglected and the last one may therefore be in error.

Water between 32° and 212° F.

Temperature Fahr	Heat units per lb.	Weight lb. per cu. ft.	Temperature Fahr	Heat units per lb.	Weight lb. per cu. ft.	Temperature Fahr	Heat units per lb.	Weight lb. per cu. ft.
32°	0.00	62.42	123	91.09	61.68	169	137.46	60.79
35	3.02	62.42	124	92.10	61.67	170	138.46	60.77
40	8.06	62.42	125	93.10	61.65	171	139.47	60.75
45	13.08	62.42	126	94.11	61.63	172	140.48	60.73
50	18.10	62.41	127	95.12	61.61	173	141.49	60.70
52	20.11	62.40	128	96.13	61.60	174	142.50	60.68
54	22.11	62.40	129	97.14	61.58	175	143.50	60.66
56	24.11	62.39	130	98.14	61.56	176	144.51	60.64
58	26.12	62.38	131	99.15	61.54	177	145.52	60.62
60	28.12	62.37	132	100.16	61.52	178	146.53	60.59
62	30.12	62.36	133	101.17	61.51	179	147.54	60.57
64	32.12	62.35	134	102.18	61.49	180	148.54	60.55
66	34.12	62.34	135	103.18	61.47	181	149.55	60.53
68	36.12	62.33	136	104.19	61.45	182	150.56	60.50
70	38.11	62.31	137	105.20	61.43	183	151.57	60.48
72	40.11	62.30	138	106.21	61.41	184	152.58	60.46
74	42.11	62.23	139	107.22	61.39	185	153.58	60.44
76	44.11	62.27	140	108.22	61.37	186	154.59	60.41
78	46.10	62.25	141	109.23	61.36	187	155.60	60.39
80	48.09	62.23	142	110.24	61.34	188	156.61	60.37
82	50.08	62.21	143	111.25	61.32	189	157.62	60.34
84	52.07	62.19	144	112.26	61.30	190	158.62	60.32
86	54.06	62.17	145	113.26	61.28	191	159.63	60.29
88	56.05	62.15	146	114.27	61.26	192	160.63	60.27
90	58.04	62.13	147	115.28	61.24	193	161.64	60.25
92	60.03	62.11	148	116.29	61.22	194	162.65	60.22
94	62.02	62.00	149	117.30	61.20	195	163.66	60.20
96	64.01	62.07	150	118.30	61.18	196	164.66	60.17
98	66.01	62.05	151	119.31	61.16	197	165.67	60.15
100	68.01	62.02	152	120.32	61.14	198	166.68	60.12
102	70.00	62.00	153	121.33	61.12	199	167.69	60.10
104	72.00	61.97	154	122.34	61.10	200	168.70	60.07
106	74.00	61.95	155	123.34	61.08	201	169.70	60.05
108	76.00	61.92	156	124.35	61.06	202	170.71	60.02
110	78.00	61.89	157	125.36	61.04	203	171.72	60.00
112	80.00	61.86	158	126.37	61.02	204	172.73	59.97
113	81.01	61.84	159	127.38	61.00	205	173.74	59.95
114	82.02	61.83	160	128.38	60.98	206	174.74	59.92
115	83.02	61.82	161	129.39	60.96	207	175.75	59.89
116	84.03	61.80	162	130.40	60.94	208	176.76	59.87
117	85.04	61.78	163	131.41	60.92	209	177.77	59.84
118	86.05	61.77	164	132.42	60.90	210	178.78	59.82
119	87.06	61.75	165	133.42	60.87	211	179.78	59.79
120	88.06	61.74	166	134.43	60.85	212	180.79	59.76
121	89.07	61.72	167	135.44	60.83			
122	90.08	61.70	168	136.45	60.81			

INDEX.

Alden Dynamometer................Page	16
Barrel Calorimeter................	38-40
Barrus Calorimeter................	47-52
Belts, Testing................	25-29
Boilers, Testing................	53-66
Standard Method................	55-64
Short Method................	65-66
Calorimeters, Barrel................	38-40
Barrus................	47-52
Separating................	44-46
Throttling................	41-43
Compression Tests................	11
Condenser, Surface................	81-82
Deflectometer................	6
Draught Gauge................	36
Duty Trial, Standard................	87-99
Dynamometers, Absorption................	15-19
Alden................	16
Calibration of................	21
Cradle................	30
Spring................	25
Transmitting................	19-25
Webber................	19-24
Engines, Testing Steam................	80-86
Pumping................	87-99
Evaporation, Equivalent................	53
Factors of................	54
Extensometers, Autographic................	5
Ordinary................	4
Feed Water, Temperature................	87
Weight of................	88-90
Gas Analysis................	60
Gauges, Draft................	36

Gauges, Steam	33
Calibration of	33-35
Indicated Horse Power	77
Indicator, Calibration of	68-70
Care of	68
Description	67
Diagrams	77-79
Reducing Motions	71
Use of	72
Leakage Test of Pump	95-96
Manometers	36
Planimeter, Polar	
Directions for Use	73
Theory of	74-76
Prony Brake	15
Pumping Engines	
Standard Duty Trial	87-99
Pumps, Testing small	100-101
Pyrometers	32
Reducing Motions	71
Separating Calorimeter	44-46
Shearing Tests	11
Specimens, Form of	7
Steam, Boilers, Testing	53-66
Consumption of	79
Engine Testing	80-86
Gauges	33
Moisture in	37
Tables	102-103
Testing Machines	3
Tests, Compression	11
Shearing	11
Tension	7-10
Transverse	11-14
Thermometers	31
Throttling Calorimeter	41-43
Transverse Tests	11-14
Valve Setting	79
Water, Table of Properties	104
Webber Dynamometer	19-24

www.ingramcontent.com/pod-product-compliance
Lightning Source LLC
Chambersburg PA
CBHW031503160426
43195CB00010BB/1090